**DRAGONBALL: EVOLUTION** THE JUNIOR NOVEL
Adapted by Stacia Deutsch and Rhody Cohon
Based on the motion picture screenplay by Ben Ramsey

Design: Carolina Ugalde

Published by VIZ Media, LLC
P.O. Box 77010
San Francisco, CA 94107

www.viz.com
www.vizkids.com

Library of Congress Cataloging-in-Publication Data

Deutsch, Stacia.
 Dragonball evolution : the junior novel / adapted by Stacia Deutsch and Rhody Cohon; based on the
original screenplay by Ben Ramsey.
    p. cm.
 ISBN-13: 978-1-4215-2664-5
 ISBN-10: 1-4215-2664-6
 I. Cohon, Rhody. II. Ramsey, Ben. III. Dragonball evolution (Motion picture) IV. Title.

 PZ7.D4953Ds 2009
 [Fic]--dc22
                        2008020233

Printed in the U.S.A.
First printing, February 2009

## The Junior Novel

**By Stacia Deutsch & Rhody Cohon**

**Screenplay by Ben Ramsey**
**Based upon the graphic novel series "Dragonball" by Akira Toriyama**

**VIZ MEDIA**
SAN FRANCISCO

# CHAPTER ONE

A drop of sweat worked its way past a pair of piercing blue eyes that burned with intensity. The bead of perspiration rolled from the boy's forehead down the tip of his nose. His eyes crossed as he watched the small drop of sweat. The droplet moved slowly at first, picking up speed as it finally fell from Goku's face and smashed with a small explosion into the dirt below.

Goku was standing on two wires, usually used to hang laundry. The wires were high and strung tightly between two wooden poles. He was precariously balanced, one foot on each wire. Goku was trying to be very, very still.

A small bug caught Goku's attention. It was crawling along the taut wire, inching toward his feet, but Goku was unwilling to move. This was his daily workout. He was learning the skills he'd need to survive: Balance. Power. Focus. And patience.

"The first rule is there are no rules," an old man's voice warned.

Goku had heard that warning before. He knew what it meant. And he was ready.

Another drop of perspiration slid across his face. He was breathing heavily. Goku caught a glimpse of himself in a shadow. Soaked with sweat, and yet his hair was still standing straight up in spikes. There was nothing he could do about it. Water, sweat, even extra-strength holding gel—nothing in the world would make his hair lie flat. He wished he looked like the other kids at school. Their hair was all neat and straight and...

"Don't worry about your hair," he chided himself. "Stay focused."

"The first one to touch the ground loses," Gohan announced.

Goku's grandfather might have been seventy years old, but he could still move like a kung fu expert. Looking up from where he was balanced, Goku stared deeply into his grandfather's eyes. Gohan's eyes reflected the wisdom of his years.

Gohan stood on the support pole for the laundry line. With the smallest of movements, he whipped his bow staff across his body. The rod moved faster and faster until the staff was nearly invisible.

It was time. All of Goku's training thus far had led to this moment. The battle was beginning. It was him against his master. Goku didn't like to lose!

Without another word, Gohan struck. Goku ducked, his feet perfectly balanced on the wires as he dodged the old man's blows.

Goku used the wires under his feet as a spring board, leaping toward his grandfather. He was moving fast, just as he'd been taught. With a combination of kicks and punches, Goku had the old man weaving back and forth to avoid Goku's expert strikes.

Goku bent backwards as Gohan jabbed at him with his staff. He narrowly avoided a blow by somersaulting onto the laundry line support beams.

Now it was his grandfather's turn to be on the wires. Gohan flipped, flying backwards as Goku charged. With the ease of a master teacher, Gohan avoided Goku's punches easily, leaping back onto the supports on the opposite side.

"Prepare to eat dirt," Gohan warned his grandson as he swung his bow staff in a mighty arc, sending Goku jumping back to the wires. He struggled to keep his balance. Leaping, dodging, and flipping, Goku continued to stay on the wire, but he knew he needed to take the lead in this battle. And soon.

There! His eyes caught sight of that little bug he'd noticed before. It was barely clinging to the taut wire.

With a solid flip Goku landed, smacking the wire with his foot as he came down, sending the insect into the air. With a flick of his hand, Goku sent the insect flying directly into Gohan's mouth at the exact moment he lunged forward with his pole.

Gohan choked, caught by surprise as he swallowed the small bug. And in that second, Goku found his opening. Gohan's bow staff slowed and Goku moved in for his final blow.

Goku flipped. Using his legs like scissors, Goku caught the bow staff and tore it out of Gohan's grasp. He sent it flying into the soft soil of the vegetable garden below.

Goku was certain that he'd won the game. One last kick and his grandpa would fall to the garden, joining his staff in the dirt. Using the wires like a springboard, Goku bounced up into a powerful flying side-kick.

But Gohan, more experienced, was prepared. With his arms and legs poised, he formed the Shadow Crane Strike. A single hand pushed out from his chest. The air rippled around them as the power from Gohan's Ki , his energy force, struck the flying boy.

Goku was knocked out of the air. His grandfather

never even touched him.

Goku fell into the soft earth of the vegetable garden, head crashing against a melon. His grandfather leapt down from the laundry line and came over to help him up.

"Shadow Crane Strike," Gohan said, as he reached over to dust the dirt off Goku. "You fell for it again."

Goku wiped melon seeds from the side of his face. "It's not easy to block a move that I can't see."

"Goku, you rely too much on your external senses." The old man shook his head. "To see, to hear, to touch. All overrated. True power comes from inside." Gohan placed his aged, gnarled hand against Goku's chest. "Your Ki is your best defense and your greatest weapon." He tapped against Goku's heart, indicating his very center. "Feel it here."

Goku felt that fighting with Ki was just too difficult. He'd rather use his muscles.

"Focus the power," Gohan taught him.

Goku humored his grandfather with a half-hearted attempt to use his Ki. Raising his hand, palm facing outward, he pushed forward, imitating Gohan. Nothing happened.

Goku looked at Gohan. "See?"

"To use your Ki," Gohan instructed, "you must

not only be at one with yourself, but also your enemy. Choose a point of focus." Gohan pointed to a tree in the garden. "See that tree? The tree is your enemy."

Goku sighed, closing his eyes.

"Use your Ki. Channel the energy through you," Gohan instructed.

He tried. He really did. But nothing happened. A breeze swept through the tree's leaves, but that was simply the wind. Not Goku's Ki. Goku opened his eyes.

"Sorry, Grandpa. I didn't feel a thing." Goku shrugged.

"Someday, Goku," Gohan said with a small nod.

Goku laughed. "Yeah," he said. "Someday I'll beat you."

Gohan grinned wildly. "Yes. It will be something to tell your friends. Beating up on a seventy-year-old man."

Goku stopped laughing and gave a sad smile. "What friends?" His mood turned sour. "Everyone at school treats me like I'm nothing, Grandpa. Less than nothing. The jocks, the brains, the rockers. I don't fit into any group."

Gohan placed an arm around his grandson. "You're special, Goku."

"No." Goku pulled out of his grandfather's grasp and stepped away. His cheeks were flushed red with anger. "I'm different. I know it. Everybody knows it." He kicked a rock. "Sometimes...they push me too far, I want to explode. I could tear them apart with one hand..."

Concern showed in Gohan's eyes. "I don't train you to fight with boys."

Tension grew in Goku. His voice rose when he asked, "Then why am I doing this?! You made me promise not to fight, okay...then..." He was on a roll now. "Teach me something I can use. Like how to get a girl. Teach me how to talk to them without stumbling all over myself. Teach me how to be normal."

Gohan spoke in a calm and steady manner, leveling his eyes at the struggling boy. "Normal is also overrated. You have to have faith in who you are."

Goku turned away from his grandfather. He felt like the old man didn't understand how hard it was for him to be different.

Gohan tried to cheer him up. He reached into his pocket and pulled out a small, wrapped package. "Happy eighteenth birthday. You think I forgot?"

Goku relaxed, then smiled, turning back to the old man. His grandfather never forgot. Goku took the package and eagerly tore off the brown paper.

Inside was a small ball. The surface was smooth, pearl-like, but with a milky translucence that gave it depth. Four stars appeared to float inside the ball. Goku rolled the ball around in his hand, curious as to what it meant.

"Sushinchu is yours," Gohan told him.

"What is it?" Goku asked. He was intrigued, but so far unimpressed.

"It's a Dragon Ball," Gohan explained. "Sushinchu means four stars. In the entire world there are only six others. From one to seven stars. Besides you, Goku, it is my only treasure."

"What does it do?" Goku continued to turn the ball over and over, searching for its meaning.

"By itself, nothing," his grandfather said. "But together, it is said the seven Dragon Balls will grant the holder one perfect wish."

Goku nodded. Sometimes he thought his grandfather was a little odd. This was one of those times. A Dragon Ball. Whatever.

Gohan reached over to wrap Goku's hand around the Dragon Ball, conveying its importance.

"Keep it safe. Always," Gohan said. It was not so much a directive as a warning.

"Thanks, Grandpa." Goku slipped the Dragon Ball into his pocket. If it was important to his grandfather, he'd take care of the thing.

"You're a man now!" Gohan cheered, lightening the mood. "After school tonight, you and me, we celebrate! I'll cook all your favorites!"

# CHAPTER TWO

Goku weaved his scooter through the traffic in the school parking lot, looking for a space. His scooter had seen better days. It was beat up and barely drove, but it was the only transportation Goku had.

There! Right in the front of the high school lot. The perfect spot.

Goku pulled into the space and just as he was flipping the kickstand down, the roar of another engine attracted his attention.

A speedster was whipping around the parking lot, and the next thing Goku knew, the car pulled into the exact same spot. Goku barely had time to dive out of the way. The speedster rolled right over his scooter and was now parked on top of Goku's ride.

Carey Fuller stepped out of the car. Goku knew Fuller and didn't like anything about him. He acted like he owned the school. And the sorry part was that in many ways he did. Carey Fuller was popular in ways

Goku only dreamed of.

Fuller barely acknowledged Goku, who was still lying on the ground.

"Hey, Fuller," Goku called out as he picked himself up. "You just wrecked my scooter." Goku had had enough of being run over, literally, by Carey Fuller and his posse.

Fuller pretended not to hear Goku. He turned to one of his buddies, a big football player named Agundes.

"Agundes," Fuller yelled out. "Did you fart? I thought I heard something."

With a snicker, Agundes nodded toward Goku. "No man, the squeak you heard is coming from him."

By then, a small crowd had gathered to see what was going on. At Agundes's remark, everyone started laughing.

Everyone except Goku. His anger rose to the surface.

"You're gonna pay for that, Fuller," Goku warned.

Just then, the school warning bell rang. Kids began leaving the parking lot, crowding like a herd of cattle into the school building.

Goku didn't move.

Fuller and his friends stayed too.

Fuller pinned Goku with a threatening stare. "Make

me pay, Geeko. I'll even give you a free shot."

Goku's hand balled into a fist. He squeezed it tight, trembling in anger. He tried to hold back.

"You started it," Fuller taunted Goku. "I'll end it. Come on, show me what you got." And with that Fuller pushed Goku, trying to prod him into action.

Goku fought every instinct within himself in order to remain passive.

After a few seconds, he looked away from Fuller, backing down from the confrontation. His jaw felt tight, his muscles tense.

Carey Fuller simply sneered. "You lift one finger, Geeko, and I'll stomp you like a bug."

From behind the circle of Fuller's buddies, a girl called out, "Carey, I'm gonna be late for class."

Fuller turned from Goku toward a beautiful, spunky girl standing and tapping her foot impatiently by the sidewalk.

It was Chi Chi. Goku wished she hadn't seen him back down from the fight. He wished she had seen him act strong and macho. Maybe then she'd like him better than Carey Fuller. He was humiliated to act so weak in front of her.

Fuller glared at Goku one last time and snarled, "There better not be a scratch on my car from your piece of junk scooter." And with that, he stepped away from Goku and wrapped his arm possessively around Chi-Chi's shoulders. They headed off to class together without a backwards glance.

As they walked away, Goku couldn't help but notice that when Fuller leaned in toward Chi Chi for a kiss, she subtly turned away.

Goku's anger at Fuller was intense. His rage touched the very depth of his soul.

The school bell rang again and Goku was now completely alone in the parking lot. He bent down to retrieve his scooter, but it was stuck. Only one part of the handlebar was visible from underneath the roadster.

Breathing deeply, Goku gathered his strength. He secured his grip on the car and lifted it a few inches off the ground.

The screech of the car's alarm shocked Goku. But more, it was the flash from a camera built into the rear view mirror of the car that got to him. Goku put the car back down.

A mechanized voice rang out: "Intrusion Alert! Warning, your image will be uploaded to local law enforcement agencies unless you step away from the vehicle immediately!"

In frustration, Goku kicked Fuller's car, but the sound of the alarm and the constant snapping of photos was too much to bear.

With a final sigh, Goku stepped away from the vehicle. He'd been defeated again.

Mr. Kingery, Goku's science teacher, was in the middle of a lecture about the upcoming solar eclipse.

The teacher stood at the front of the room, pointing to an image on a screen. "This is an astronomical phenomenon known as a complete solar eclipse," he droned. "In two weeks' time, we will all have the opportunity to experience this rare phenomenon ourselves. What causes eclipses?"

Goku sank down in his chair, trying to become invisible. The only reason he went to this class was because Chi Chi was in it too.

He stood his textbook up as a cover from the teacher and covertly stared at Chi Chi sitting two rows away. It always seemed that there was some sort of soft light surrounding her.

While Goku stared at Chi Chi, a chubby know-it-all named Weaver answered Mr. Kingery's question. Goku was so busy checking out Chi Chi, he barely heard

Weaver's reply.

"A solar eclipse is caused by the moon blocking the sun from the earth." Weaver was right. Of course.

"Correct!" Mr. Kingery exclaimed. "From the dawn of civilization, superstitions have marked solar eclipses as the sign of the apocalypse." He went on, saying, "In India, the eclipse symbolizes Rahu, the demon of darkness, devouring the sun. The Chinese believe eclipses are caused by a dragon trying to swallow the sun. The eclipse marked the beginning of the end."

Whatever else Mr. Kingery had to say was lost to Goku as he began to daydream about Chi Chi sitting in a field of flowers, eating wild strawberries...

SLAM! Mr. Kingery's wooden pointer crashed down on Goku's desktop, jolting him from his daydream.

"Goku," Mr. Kingery addressed him. "What might our ancestors say about the upcoming solar eclipse?"

Goku flipped through his textbook, desperate to find the right answer. He looked around the classroom, hopeful that someone, anyone, would help. No one would even meet his eyes. He was on his own.

"Uh," Goku stammered, searching for the right answer. "My grandfather would say beware of the Nameks."

Mr. Kingery looked puzzled. "Nameks?" he asked.

"They're an alien race that almost destroyed Earth two thousand years ago—" Goku was suddenly aware that the entire class was looking at him like he was a freak.

Mr. Kingery simply smiled. "Well," he said. "Let's hope it doesn't happen again."

Everyone laughed. Goku's face flushed red with embarrassment. Would he ever fit in?

Between classes, there was a mad rush of students going from one room to another. The students were all grabbing books, papers, and pencils from their lockers which were opened with the swipe of an ID card in a card reader.

Goku had just grabbed stuff for his next class and was about to head off when he noticed that Chi Chi was having trouble with the card reader on her locker.

She repeatedly swiped her card, but the red light continued blinking. No green light would appear. Her friend Emi was shaking her head, as if she completely understood.

"I hate those things," Emi said, pointing at Chi Chi's ID card. "They never work and," she held up her own card, "just look at my picture. Ugh." Even from where Goku was lurking around the corner he could see that

Emi was right. The photo was horrible.

Chi Chi hit the locker with her fist impatiently. "I've got a paper due next period and it's stuck in there."

The class bell rang. Emi grabbed her books and slammed her own locker shut. She sympathetically mouthed "gotta go" before rushing off to class, leaving Chi Chi to deal with the stuck locker on her own.

Chi Chi was now banging at her locker, desperate to get it open. Moving away from the safety of the shadows, Goku took a step forward, ready to help, but then he stopped. He was petrified. Goku took a deep breath then eased back away from Chi Chi.

He continued to watch her struggle, wondering if he would find the courage to offer his help.

Chi Chi was beyond frustrated. She pulled repeatedly on the handle, until she hurt her hand. She grumbled under her breath, shaking away the pain.

Goku looked around at the now empty hallway, concentrating. He focused his energy in his chest just like his grandfather Gohan had shown him. Slowly, he raised his hand, palm out.

Goku surprised himself. When he pressed his hand slightly forward, the entire wall of lockers on Chi Chi's side of the hallway popped open. Contents from every locker tumbled out onto the floor.

Goku was shocked that using his Ki actually worked! It didn't work perfectly, but...

Chi Chi turned, rotating quickly on one heel to see who had just opened all the lockers in the hall. She discovered Goku standing a ways away, his palm still raised, facing her.

Uncertain what to do or say, Goku dropped his eyes from Chi Chi's penetrating stare and quickly began to walk away.

"Stop!" Chi Chi called after him. He froze. "Hey... Goku, right?"

Goku turned to face her and lifted his eyes to hers.

"Did you do that?" Chi Chi asked, waving her hand across the hall indicating the open lockers.

Goku had trouble finding his voice. "Uh...yeah, it was something my grandpa taught me."

"You used your Ki." Chi Chi grinned at Goku and he felt his heart melt.

"You know about Ki?" he asked, once he could get it together to speak.

"Just because my name is Chi Chi doesn't make me a complete idiot," she responded with a laugh.

Goku replied, "Right, there's lots more stupider names than Chi Chi...not that Chi Chi is stupid...I mean, it's not normal, but normal is overrated...not saying you're stupid or overrated..." He smacked his forehead with the palm of his hand and groaned. "I'm gonna stop talking now." Deciding to cut his losses, Goku turned and headed off toward his next class without another word.

Chi Chi called after him again. "Hey," she said to his retreating form. "I'm having a party tonight at my house."

Goku stopped in his tracks. He couldn't help but smile. "I'll be there."

# CHAPTER THREE

Gohan hummed as he prepared Goku's birthday dinner. He'd chopped fresh vegetables from their garden and was frying them in a gigantic wok. Blazing flames licked the side of the cast iron half-dome as he tossed marinated chicken feet into the mix.

"I got chicken feet!" he announced to Goku, who was upstairs in his room. "Couldn't find good swallow's tongue, but the squabs were fat. You want those with or without the heads?"

No answer.

Gohan opened the oven. "Mmm," he sighed with pleasure as the scent of the golden brown roasting squabs filled the room. He'd left the heads attached, for now.

Careful not to burn himself, Gohan picked up a particularly nasty-looking chicken foot and shoved it completely into his mouth, taste-testing his cooking. When he pulled the foot back out, only the bones remained.

"Dinner's almost ready," he called up to Goku. "Five minutes!" Gohan continued to putter in the kitchen, clearly enjoying the preparations for his grandson's birthday meal.


Upstairs, Goku slipped a brand new shirt over his head and tucked it into his pants. He was getting ready for Chi Chi's party.

Looking in the mirror, he thought the outfit worked. The problem was, of course, his hair. Yep, like always, it was sticking straight up in spikes.

Goku grabbed a bottle of extra-firm hair gel. He squeezed out a huge gob of the sticky stuff and plastered it on his hair, slicking it back. He admired his work in the mirror; his hair looked great.

TANG! With a reverberating ping, like the popping of a spring, his hair sprang back up. He looked like he had porcupine spikes on his head.

He'd have tried again, but he knew it was no use. Grabbing his wallet and throwing his school pants on the bed, Goku took one last peek in the mirror then was ready to take off.

Just as he was about to leave, the gift from his grandfather, the Dragon Ball, slipped out of his discarded pants' pocket and rolled onto his covers. He saw the ball, and for a split second was unsure if he should leave it or take it with him. His grandfather had told him to keep it safe, so he snatched it up and after slipping it into his jacket pocket, climbed out his bedroom window and dropped two floors down to the ground outside.

After one look at his grandfather through the dining room window, Goku pushed away any guilt he might have felt and hurried off into the night.

In the kitchen, Gohan lit the last candle on Goku's birthday cake. He carried the cake into the dining room, saying, "Goku, happy birthday! Life is short, we eat dessert first!"

But Goku was nowhere to be found. Gohan turned to the stairwell and called out, "Goku?"

Holding the cake, Gohan stood alone in their country house. Puzzled. Eighteen candles silently burned for a boy who had disappeared without saying, "Goodbye."

At Chi Chi McRoberts's estate, the party was already in full swing when Goku arrived. Music blared as groups of kids moved through the gates into a courtyard.

Goku sighed when he noticed Agundes and four

other jocks standing outside the gate, leaning casually on Carey Fuller's speedster.

Goku steeled his courage and kept walking past them, toward the party.

Agundes looked up, and catching sight of Goku, asked, "What are you doing here, Geeko?" He stepped in front of Goku.

"Name's Goku. Just going to the party." Goku pressed forward, trying to step around Agundes, but Agundes's big football player pals spread out, ready for action. Goku's path was completely blocked.

"I was invited," Goku told them. "I'm not looking for trouble."

Agundes laughed. "Trouble found you, freak. So turn around, walk away. And no one's ever gonna know you were here."

Goku sighed and looked down at his feet. He might as well go back home.

As he turned to leave, Agundes and his friends sneered smugly; they knew that they'd won again.

Goku paused. "I'm not doing that anymore," he said as much to himself as to them. Turning back, Goku faced the bullies. "I made a promise I wouldn't fight," Goku told them. All he wanted was to walk past them into the party.

Agundes had a different idea. "It's not gonna be a fight," he snarled. "It'll be a massacre."

Agundes opened with a left jab. Goku's reflexes were so quick, it was almost impossible to see him move. He simply tilted his head three inches to avoid the punch. Agundes came back with a vicious punch. Again, Goku moved faster than Agundes's fist. By shifting slightly, Goku ducked and Agundes missed him completely.

Agundes's friends jumped into the action. A muscle-bound dude named Hillenbrand lunged at Goku, throwing punches as he led the others into the fight. Goku was surrounded, but not for long. He slipped out of the middle of their circle. He took down Hillenbrand with ease. Then he set his sights on Moreno who was coming to tackle him at the exact same moment that Butler was soaring toward him with a flying side-kick.

Goku's eyes flashed brightly as he side-stepped just in time. A small push redirected Butler's flying side-kick straight into Moreno's face. And a little tripping action sent Moreno straight into Butler's stomach. The two oversized bullies went down simultaneously.

Palmer was next. He came toward Goku with a mean left-right combination. Ducking and weaving, Goku backed up against a parked car. Palmer reared back, throwing everything into his final, killer punch.

Goku was ready.

Turning his body, Palmer's punch slipped by Goku, crashing into the window of the car. The glass cracked. Clutching his fist, Palmer yelled out.

"That's got to hurt," Goku said as he moved away from Palmer and the splintered window.

Goku had taken down four big jocks without a scratch on himself.

Carey Fuller came out of the courtyard to see what all the noise was about. Chi Chi was right behind him.

Fuller was beyond shocked to see his three friends flat out on the ground and Palmer holding his hand like it was broken.

Goku approached Chi Chi. "Hello, Chi Chi," he said casually. "Thanks for inviting me to the party."

Fuller looked at Chi Chi. He was obviously mad that she'd invited Goku.

Goku couldn't help himself as he said to Fuller, "Your friends have been showing me what they got." He pointed at all four of them sprawled out. "Nothing."

Face flushed red with anger, Fuller pulled away from Chi Chi and moved aggressively toward Goku. "You're dead."

"No, Carey, stop!" Chi Chi's voice pierced the cool night air.

Fuller glanced around, frantically looking for a weapon. He pulled a decorative iron rod from the nearby garden, and wielding it high over his head, made for Goku.

Goku stepped away from Fuller, backing himself against Carey's prized speedster. Enraged, Fuller charged, swinging the iron rod like a madman on fire.

It was the most basic of moves. Goku barely broke a sweat. He simply turned, avoiding the iron rod and evading the attack. Fuller's rod connected with the speedster's side mirror, knocking it right off the car.

"Close one," Goku taunted. After years of teasing, he had finally decided to face the bullies. His grandfather would probably be mad that Goku used his training to fight, but for this moment, it felt really, really good to finally stand up for himself. To prove himself. "Try again," he teased.

Fuller's car alarm went off again, making a siren's blare. This time the small camera on the rearview window was documenting Carey's every move.

"Intrusion alert! Warning, your image will be uploaded to local law enforcement agencies unless you step away from the vehicle immediately!"

Fuller screamed in rage, raising the iron rod and swinging wildly at Goku again.

In a swift, seamless move, Goku ducked, causing Fuller to smash the front windshield of his own car. The camera flashed, freezing Fuller's image of rage and uploading it to the local police.

"Nice swing," Goku commented casually. "Good form."

Fuller whipped the rod in Goku's direction. Goku jumped up on the hood, masterfully using the car as a shield. He rolled across the roof. Fuller followed, smashing at Goku with the rod, every swing from Fuller further damaging his car. The hood was dented. The side door was gashed. Windows cracked.

Gasping for breath, Fuller looked over his once beautiful car, now a total wreck. He turned to Goku, hatred in his eyes.

"You got a couple of dings here. Might try buffing it out." Goku smiled at Fuller.

Something in Fuller's eyes made Goku uneasy. He noticed Fuller was looking over Goku's shoulder. Someone must be sneaking up behind him!

Moreno and Fuller attacked at the exact same moment, both carrying matching iron garden rods. Moreno swung high. Fuller swung low.

Goku had only a split second to react. Time seemed to freeze as Fuller's swing ramped toward him from one direction, Moreno's from another.

Within an instant, Goku was moving at a speed faster than either bully could attack. His body blurred as he jumped, initiating a back flip.

Fuller's rod missed Goku by mere inches.

Moreno's rod soared over Goku's head, but he missed as Goku's body twisted in the air.

Without a scratch, Goku landed on the roof of Fuller's car. He stood back, safely out of the way, while Fuller and Moreno slammed into each other. They both slumped to the ground in a groaning heap.

Goku stood on top of Fuller's battered car, barely winded. He'd done it. He'd faced Fuller and his bullies and had won! A new feeling swelled up inside him. It was joy, pure joy.

Chi Chi was staring up at him. Smiling.

This was going to be a great birthday. The best one ever.

# CHAPTER FOUR

Goku's birthday cake was ruined. The candles had burned all the way down.

Gohan sat on his bamboo mat in the center of the living room, legs folded beneath, meditating. He felt like he'd aged in the time Goku had been gone. Now he waited patiently for his grandson to return and explain himself.

A shadow passed behind the curtains. Did he detect a slight movement coming from somewhere between the floor and back door? The old man could feel it in his bones. He glanced around. Someone lurked outside the country house.

Unfortunately, Gohan's bow staff was just out of reach and there was no time to retrieve it.

Suddenly, the front door burst open. There stood a mysterious and beautiful woman in her late twenties, dressed in gleaming red. She had short hair and would have looked quite fashionable, except for the massive amount of weapons strapped all over her body.

Gohan wasn't blinded by her beauty. He immediately knew she was dangerous, and that it would take all his power to fight her.

Without a word of warning she whipped half a dozen shuriken throwing knives toward the old man. The knives sliced through the air, their razor sharp blades glinting in the moonlight.

Gohan moved like lightning. Leaping up from his meditation mat and picking up the bow staff, it quickly became a blur in his hands. He knocked the blades to the ground, one after the next.

Gohan stood, holding his staff at the ready, as if to say, "Is that all you've got?"

Behind the woman, another form appeared. An imposing, bald figure moved out of the shadows into the room. His skin had a greenish hue, his ears slightly pointed, and his face was lined with bitterness and pain. This man's fearsome power was obvious.

The new figure stared at the old man for a heartbeat then announced to the woman, "Let's go, Mai. It's not here." Without another word, he closed his hand into a fist, and the country house began to shake.

Gohan was ready for a fight, but not like this. Everything that wasn't bolted down began to rattle and fall to the ground.

An invisible force was taking over and Gohan had no power against it. He dropped to his knees, his entire body tense. Sweat poured out of the old man.

The two figures turned and swept out of the house, leaving as quickly as they had come.

In the quiet moonlit night, the house crumbled as if a powerful force had crushed it in the palm of its hand. Then, as the fierce twosome disappeared into the darkness the crumbling house exploded, leaving nothing behind but a pile of rubble and a cloud of dust.

Inside the courtyard of the McRoberts's estate, Goku and Chi Chi were hidden away in a darkened corner. Soft music played as Chi Chi reached over to take Goku's hand in hers.

"You've never done this before, have you?" Chi Chi asked, looking down at their intertwined fingers.

"Sure," Goku said, pretending like she didn't make him completely nervous. "Many times...in my head."

"You're different," Chi Chi said with a laugh.

Goku didn't want to be different. He wanted to fit in.

Chi Chi felt tension creep into his hand, realized what she had said and changed her statement. "I like different. I know it's hard to believe, but we're a lot alike. There are things I do that nobody knows about…" Her words dropped off as she snuggled in a little closer.

"This is the best birthday I've ever had," Goku remarked, enjoying her closeness.

"Today is your birthday?" Chi Chi asked, squeezing his hand in hers.

Goku glanced down at his watch. "Actually…right now. Ever since I can remember, my grandpa and I celebrated my birthday at the exact same time. He calls it my grand entrance."

Inside Goku's jacket pocket, the Dragon Ball began to glow, but Goku didn't notice. He was too wrapped up in Chi Chi's next question.

"What happened to your parents?"

Goku shook his head and answered honestly. "I don't know. My grandpa said everything will be explained when I turn eighteen."

All of a sudden, a bad feeling came over Goku. Goosebumps broke out all over his neck and he shivered.

Something drew him to look up at the moon. It looked somehow different. Strange. Blue and bright with blinding intensity. And then, it flashed. The moon ignited with green flames, emerald energy shot toward Goku.

He shook his head to clear this vision. No. He'd imagined it. The moon looked normal and Chi Chi clearly hadn't noticed anything odd.

And yet, the feeling of dread was so overwhelming, he couldn't think straight.

"Something's wrong," he said.

"Yeah. I know," Chi Chi remarked, totally oblivious. "I've never felt this way about anyone else before." She leaned in closer to him, but Goku backed away.

"No, Chi Chi," he told her. "Something's wrong with my grandpa."

"What?" she asked, voice sounding both concerned and confused.

Goku pulled his hand away from hers. "He's in trouble. I...I have to go."

"Goku?"

"I'll see you later!" Goku called back at her as he hurried away, leaving Chi Chi alone under a very normal-looking, pale blue moon.

When Goku arrived home, he was shocked to discover all that remained of his house was the foundation and a few exposed beams. Dust filled the air.

"Grandpa!" Goku shouted desperately.

Goku rushed into what was left of the unstable structure. Crawling along the floor, he searched every inch of the rubble for a sign of life.

A low moan came from beyond an upturned table in what used to be the living room. Goku hurried toward the sound. Beneath a stack of furniture, there seemed to be a small space, just big enough for a man to hide.

Goku began to dig through the debris. Without warning, a loose beam crashed down toward him. He dove away, barely escaping. He furiously started digging again.

"Grandpa?" He'd found the old man. Gohan was barely breathing. His battered body was in bad shape. Goku hauled his grandfather outside and gently laid him on the soft soil of the vegetable garden. "Grandpa," he said, reluctant to leave, but knowing that he must. "I'm getting help."

"No," Gohan whispered. "Stay here with me. Not much time left." He wheezed and sputtered, laboring to stay conscious.

Tears filled Goku's eyes. "I'm sorry, Grandpa. I'm sorry I wasn't here. Who did this to you?"

"Nameks," the old man breathed. "Lord Piccolo has returned." He locked eyes with Goku. "Sushinchu is safe?"

For a second Goku was confused. But then he realized what his grandfather was talking about. Reaching into his jacket pocket, Goku pulled out the Dragon Ball. It was glowing translucent. The four stars within, flowing freely.

When the old man looked up at Goku, this time there was fear in his eyes. "It has begun."

Goku fixated on the Dragon Ball. He could not seem to pull his gaze away. The stars, captured within the ball, were hypnotizing him. They pulsated as they glowed.

The vision came to Goku in a quick burst of form and color:

A large asteroid. Totally engulfed in flames from entry into the atmosphere. The rock plows into the earth, burrowing itself into the ground. A flash in the cracked, burning rock reveals a monstrous red eye. The eye slowly opens...

Startled by the images, Goku dropped the Dragon Ball into the dirt. The glow faded as the ball settled on the ground.

Gohan's rasping breaths brought Goku back to reality. "Find Master Roshi," Gohan instructed, each breath becoming more and more difficult. "...In Paozu...tell him...Piccolo has returned...he will know what to do…" Gohan's lungs filled with fluid and he coughed wildly. Goku could see that his grandpa was losing his life force.

Gohan was struggling to tell Goku something. By the pain on his face, Goku could tell it was important. He leaned in to listen:

"Seven Dragon Balls must be found
For all men's fate will be bound
To battle forces of death and fear
And compel Shen Long to appear…"

Gohan was so weak. Goku took his grandfather's hand in his. "Grandfather, stop. You have to rest."

Gohan tightened his hand around Goku's. He looked into Goku's eyes and said, "Goku, you must find the Dragon Balls. Before the eclipse. I'm sorry. I cannot join you on this journey. Remember to always have faith in who you are."

Gohan released his last breath. Overcome with grief, Goku bowed his head.

A dirt mound marked the grave of Gohan on the top of the hillside. Beautiful round rocks outlined the perimeter. Goku dug another hole at the head of the grave. There, he planted a small tree as the headstone. With a pail of water, Goku nourished the tree's life amongst the dead.

Goku stood over his beloved grandfather, knowing what he must do.

He had a mission.

To talk to Master Roshi. To find all seven Dragon Balls.

When the sun rose, Goku would set out for Paozu.

# CHAPTER FIVE

At dawn, Goku moved cautiously through the remains of his home, wondering what force could possibly have caused the massive destruction. In what used to be the kitchen, a plate of squab with beaks opened in a silent cry remained incredibly untouched. What was once supposed to be a delicious birthday dinner was a reminder to Goku of his guilt for having left his grandfather alone.

Very little was left of the house or its contents. Goku was overwhelmed by all the damage. In Gohan's room, only one thing appeared to have survived: an old iron chest at the foot of what once was Gohan's bed.

Goku had never opened the chest before. He'd seen it, of course, but the chest was private. The things inside belonged solely to his grandfather and he'd respected that. Now, with Gohan gone, Goku moved to the chest and gingerly lifted the lid.

Inside, neatly folded, was a pristine orange gi. The

suit of a great master.

Goku took the gi out of the chest and gently touched the fabric. Holding the gi gave him a connection to his grandfather. He felt close to the old man once again.

A noise outside startled him, and he quickly put the gi back into the chest and quietly went to investigate.

Goku hid in the shadows, behind a wall, in a collapsed section of the room. From there, he had a clear view of the ground floor.

Someone was walking through the house. Goku watched the figure, barely containing his rage. He wondered if he might be about to face the person who killed his grandfather and left their home in ruins.

Keeping to the shadows, Goku moved stealthily toward the fallen beams where he'd last seen the intruder. Striking an offensive pose, he readied himself for a confrontation.

When Goku leapt into the room, no one was there. But within a second, a bright red dot appeared on Goku's forehead. He knew immediately that he'd been tricked. No matter how good his combat skills were, there was no way Goku could fight against a laser-guided, high-tech weapon.

"Where is it?" A pretty but intense girl in her twenties demanded. "I know it's here." She shifted her gun hand slightly. The laser now focused directly between Goku's eyes.

Goku wasn't afraid. "Are you Piccolo?" he asked her.

"No." She didn't lower the gun. "My name's Bulma."

"Did you kill my grandfather?" Goku asked, unsure how he'd react if the answer was "Yes."

But it wasn't. "Listen, idiot," Bulma was practically shouting, annoyed. "If I was a Piccolo, whatever that is, I wouldn't tell you. And if I killed your grandfather, I would have shot you by now." She didn't lower her gun. "Somebody stole the Promethium Orb and I'm here to get it back."

With her free hand, Bulma pulled out a handheld device with a radar grid. She activated the locator. It beeped, blinking wildly.

"You have it!" she declared, eyes flashing angrily. Bulma tightened her grip on her weapon.

Goku refused to stand there any longer with Bulma's weapon pointed at his head. In a swift move, he leapt out of her line of fire. Bulma shot the gun. Goku dove away.

The gun blast missed him, but in the chaos as he tumbled, the Dragon Ball flew out of his jacket pocket.

Goku performed a nearly perfect spinning back kick, dislodging the gun from Bulma's hand.

But Bulma was prepared. As the gun flew from Bulma's right hand, her left arm whipped out another weapon from a mechanical slide.

The Dragon Ball thumped to the floor, rolling between them. They both dove for it. Bulma got there first. She jumped back from Goku, raised her new weapon immediately, and trained it on Goku's forehead.

"Nice move," she told him. "But I'm not gonna miss again. My father found this Promethium Orb twenty years ago. You stole it from me last night. I'm not leaving here without it."

Goku looked at Bulma intently. "I don't know what you're talking about. That is a Dragon Ball. Sushinchu, four-star ball. I promised my grandfather to keep it safe. No one is going to take it from me." He bent his knees slightly, preparing to do whatever it would take to get back the Dragon Ball.

Bulma paused. "Did you say four stars?" She breathed deeply, shaking her head. "The Promethium Orb has five stars."

"Who's the idiot?" Goku smirked. "Look at it."

Bulma checked out the Dragon Ball. Goku watched her counting the stars. "Oh, my goodness!" she declared, horrified. "I could have killed you!"

"You weren't even close," Goku said with a confident smile.

Bulma looked up at him, but only for a second. Her attention was centered on Sushinchu. "I knew it," she declared, rolling the Dragon Ball over in her hand. "There are others."

"Seven to be exact," Goku told her.

Bulma opened her palm to reveal Goku's Dragon Ball. "What do you want for this one?" she asked.

"It's not for sale." Goku snatched the Dragon Ball back from her.

"Everybody's got a price," Bulma informed him, keeping one eye on the Dragon Ball.

"Not me," Goku responded. "What happened to your Dragon Ball?"

"A thief broke into my father's company, the Capsule Corporation." She drifted into memory as she told the story. "Someone hacked a third-level secured vault and stole the Promethium, I mean, Dragon Ball. There's no way I would let it go without a fight."

Bulma had been there when the break-in occurred. She'd seen the thief ignite a jet pack, and Bulma had fired her gun. But it was no use. The thief rocketed through a skylight, escaping with the Dragon Ball.

"I swore to my father I'd get it back," Bulma told Goku. "I followed the signal here. That's when I ran into you." She paused. "Sorry I fired on you. I thought you were a thief."

Goku laughed. "I'm just lucky you weren't a better shot." Then he asked, "How did you know I have a Dragon Ball?"

"Look at this." Bulma showed Goku a small hand-held gadget with a high-tech screen. "I invented it. This little machine can detect and locate the signature wavelength emitted by the Dragon Balls." She turned the screen so Goku could see and activated the device.

When placed next to Goku's Dragon Ball, the locator went crazy. The radar grid flashed and beeped.

Goku was impressed. "You made a Dragon Ball energy locator."

"Dragon Ball Energy," Bulma repeated the phrase. "DBE. That's a catchy name. I've been calling it a Promethium Energy Extractor."

"PEE?" Goku chuckled. "That's nasty. Are you some kind of scientist?"

"I have a Ph.D. in Applied Dynamics with a minor in Tactical Weaponry." She paused for Goku's reaction. He gave none. So she went on, "I'm close to a breakthrough. I can feel it. The key must be the other Dragon

Balls." Her expression cleared as Bulma became certain what she needed to do. "I have to get them all," she declared.

"What good will the Dragon Balls do you?" Goku asked, curious about the look on Bulma's face.

"They're gonna make me famous!"

Goku didn't believe her.

Bulma explained. "Who invented the light bulb?"

"Thomas Edison," Goku replied, rolling his eyes. "Everybody knows that."

"When I harness the energy of the Dragon Balls, it will become an unlimited source of electricity. Then everyone will remember my name: Bulma Enchanto."

At that announcement, Goku couldn't help but laugh.

"What's so funny?" Bulma asked, her hands on her hips.

"You're right. No one's gonna forget your name." Now that he knew her name, he finally introduced himself. "I'm Goku. Maybe we can help each other. I need to find Master Roshi in Paozu. Take me there and I'll help you find the Dragon Balls."

"I have a DBE. Why would I need you?" Bulma was obviously used to working alone.

Goku pointed out the destroyed house. "Somebody

else is looking for them," he informed her. "You might need back-up."

"Good point," Bulma agreed. Then, extending a hand, she accepted Goku's offer. He shook her hand and the deal was sealed. They were going to seek out the seven Dragon Balls together.

Bulma placed an eggplant-shaped capsule on the ground. With a remote control, she punched a button and pulled Goku back as the capsule began to open. Mechanical shapes unfolded like origami and in a matter of moments a high-tech speedster was formed.

Bulma started the engine while Goku rushed back to the house to collect a few things. When Goku returned, he was carrying a backpack and his grandfather's bow staff.

"You know this is going to be dangerous." Goku wanted her to understand. "We're going up against an unknown enemy who has already killed my grandfather. It'll be a miracle if we come out of this alive."

Bulma just patted Goku's place on the bike seat behind her. "Stop selling. You had me at 'dangerous.'"

Goku smiled as he climbed onto the back of the roadster. They roared off.

In a distant jungle, a native village leader fell dead to the ground. His expression was frozen in a scream as white foam dripped from his mouth. The leader wore a beautifully strung necklace made with precious stones. In the middle of the necklace hung the seven-starred Dragon Ball.

A powerful hand reached out and grabbed the Dragon Ball, snapping it off the dead man's necklace. Lord Piccolo was pleased with himself. He held the Dragon Ball high, showing it off to his evil assistant, Mai.

"I told you he would give it to me," Lord Piccolo announced, and without another glance at the dead man, he used the power of his fist to set the entire area on fire.

Above the decimated trees, and high above the blazing inferno, an airship hovered over the tragic site.

"Our ride is here," Mai said to Piccolo. They boarded the airship and headed off on their own quest to collect the Dragon Balls.

# CHAPTER SIX

Bulma and Goku raced on the speedster, passing a broken sign atop a rusted pole. It read: "Welcome to Paozu, City of Tomorrow."

They didn't stop until they reached the center of town. Bulma parked the bike next to an information kiosk. Goku looked around. The city had clearly seen better days. Storefronts were shuttered. The street was nearly empty.

Bulma walked over to the information kiosk where an avatar smiled and asked, "How can I help you?" in a pleasant voice.

Bulma spent a few minutes talking to the avatar. When she walked away, she had downloaded the city's directory into her handheld screen.

She came back and sat next to Goku, who was ravenously eating a sandwich. Bulma lifted her bike goggles, revealing deep dust circles around her eyes. She looked like a raccoon. Bulma and Goku were both travel-weary and incredibly dirty.

While Goku ate, Bulma scrolled through the names on her handheld device. "I've tried every possible spelling of Roshi in the directory. He's not listed."

"Did you try Master?" Goku asked, mouth full of sandwich.

Bulma simply stared at Goku like he'd gone crazy.

Goku swallowed. "M...A...S..."

She cut him off. "I know how to spell 'Master.' He's not going to be listed under 'Master.'"

Suddenly Goku knew there was no need to search further. "He's here."

"How do you know?" Bulma asked, her eyes squinting in the same direction Goku was looking.

Goku gobbled down the last bite of his sandwich and stood up. "I could always sense my grandfather," he explained. "I know he's gone now but I'm getting the same feeling."

A low beeping sound was coming from Bulma's shoulder bag. The two of them looked at each other, then Bulma reached hurriedly in and pulled out the DBE. Two dots were visible on the radar screen. Goku's Dragon Ball was the first dot.

Bulma was excited. "There's another Dragon Ball here!"

Night came quickly. They were so close to another Dragon Ball that Goku and Bulma decided to search for it first and then find Master Roshi. The DBE led them to a giant construction site surrounded by the lights of the city.

A crumbling shack stood in the middle of the area. A single paved road led to the home. The shack was the only thing standing between the past and the future.

Excited by the discovery of another Dragon Ball, Bulma leapt off the bike and rushed toward the shack.

"Bulma, wait!" Goku called after her. But she wasn't stopping for anything.

Goku cautiously followed Bulma.

Bulma barged her way into the shack, but stopped right inside the door. The DBE was going crazy.

Goku realized the problem when he peered in. The Dragon Ball could be hidden anywhere in the funky little shack. Piles of junk were jammed into every corner. It was a pack rat's heaven.

"We can't just break into somebody's house," Goku whispered to Bulma. He glanced around, searching the darkness for the person who lived there.

"We're not breaking in," Bulma responded. "The door was unlocked." Bulma was not going to be deterred. She held the DBE aloft and entered the house, searching for the Dragon Ball. Goku remained behind, unsure what to do.

After a few silent moments, he called her name in a soft voice. "Bulma." There was no answer. He tried again, "Bulma!" Nothing. Reluctantly, Goku stepped across the threshold.

On guard, Goku moved cautiously into the large, darkened room. He was careful not to make any noise.

"Bulma," he whispered once more. Bulma seemed to have disappeared. Annoyed, Goku turned to retrace his steps to the front door. As careful as he was, he still managed to knock into a perfectly balanced sculpture made of various metal objects.

As parts of the sculpture began to fall, Goku's hands moved like lightning. He caught random plates and boxes in midair before they smashed to the floor. Miraculously, Goku was able to save every item and gently began to return them to the sculpture.

A tiny bead then rolled off the pile. Goku, with his hands still full, could not possibly catch it, and it dropped to the floor with a small ping.

From a previously unnoticed hammock strung in the corner of the room, a figure popped up. Goku froze in his tracks. Caught. The man looked like a beggar. He was unshaven and gaunt, but his eyes burned intensely.

"Thief!" The beggar cried, jumping down from his hammock.

Goku stepped back, trying to explain, "Wait a second. It's not what you…" But before he could finish his sentence, the beggar struck with a speed so surprising and powerful that Goku could not defend himself. Goku dropped pieces of sculpture as he flew across the room and crashed into a large shelf.

"Listen old man, I don't want to hurt—" Goku began as he stood up, taking a defensive position.

But before Goku could finish his thought, or assume a fighting position, the beggar was spinning in the air. Goku managed to block the old man's right foot but the left one smashed Goku in the face. "This is not happening," Goku muttered as he slid down to the floor, dazed.

"Believe it, punk," the beggar taunted. "You're getting your clock cleaned."

Goku stood up now, rising to the challenge. "I'm not gonna hit you, but you're not touching me again," he declared.

The beggar smiled as he struck a defensive pose. Goku faced him and then experienced the fastest, most amazing series of blocks and dodges in martial arts history. Goku was stunned at how quickly the beggar could move. His hands and feet were almost a blur. Goku was glad for his grandfather's training because he could almost match the man in speed and agility.

"You both have to stop!" Bulma announced when she entered the room to find the two men fighting it out.

The beggar glanced quickly at Bulma before turning back to Goku. "You've been trained well," he complimented, before throwing another series of punches and kicks.

Goku agreed then added, "Now I'm going to end it."

The beggar attacked. Goku flipped in the air and as he flew above the man, Goku formed the Shadow Crane Strike.

Goku landed behind the beggar and thrust his open palm forward. The air popped and rippled. Noting the distorted air in front of him, the old man slid down to the floor, dodging the shock waves. The airwaves passed breezily over him, hitting Bulma instead and knocking her on her butt.

Goku hurried over to help Bulma up. The beggar, on the other hand, didn't move. He watched Goku with curious eyes, then suddenly his face broke into a big smile.

"Shadow Crane Strike! I'd recognize that anywhere. How is Gohan?" The beggar continued to grin.

Goku steadied Bulma and turned. "You knew my grandfather?"

"Knew him?" The beggar practically laughed. "I trained him."

Goku looked at the old man, the truth dawning. "You are Master Roshi."

Roshi put his hands on his hips and declared, "I am Muten-Roshi, the invincible!" He laughed the ironic laugh of a man who was once powerful, but whom life had beaten down.

Goku nodded, understanding the hard times that had befallen Master Roshi. "My grandfather is dead," he told the one-time master. "He was murdered. Before he died, he told me to find you and to tell you Piccolo has returned. He said you'd know what to do."

Goku glanced at Bulma. He guessed that they were both thinking the same thing: Roshi looked nothing like a man who would know what to do.

Goku went on. "My grandfather also told me a poem." He began with, "Seven Dragon Balls..."

Master Roshi picked up and continued the poem: "Seven Dragon Balls must be found
For all men's fate will be bound
To battle forces of death and fear
And compel Shen Long to appear..."

Bulma and Goku looked at each other.

"It was a nursery rhyme," Roshi explained. "Told to us by the ancient master. I haven't heard it in decades." The years peeled away and it was easy to see greatness lurking behind the eyes of the beggar.

"Then you probably know we have to find the Dragon Balls before the eclipse," Goku told him.

Roshi remembered. "Eclipse, of course. The blood moon..." His words trailed off as he got lost in thought.

Bulma brought the old man back to the present by asking, "Do you have a Dragon Ball?"

"Dragon Ball?" he repeated. "Yes, it's here somewhere." He moved to a trunk and began to dig through years of accumulated junk. Everything imaginable was flying out onto the floor.

While Roshi continued to search, Goku's attention was drawn to another part of the room. Something was pulling him forward. Behind a pile of ancient armor and weapons, it drew him in. He found it!

Arushinchu. The Dragon Ball with two stars.

"It's here," Goku announced, picking up the Dragon Ball.

The vision came quickly:

A demon opens his monstrous red eyes. Razor sharp fangs glisten. Sharp claws slash the air as the demon lunges forward. A sound rips from the demon's throat that can only be described as inhuman.

Goku collapsed from the vision, his hand falling to his side. Arushinchu, the two-star Dragon Ball, rolled to the floor.

Master Roshi checked on the boy and then scooped the ball up, studying the swirling stars for a long minute. "If the prophecy is true, in seven days when the sun is eclipsed by the blood moon, the apocalypse will begin."

Bulma stared at the old man in disbelief. "Don't be crazy," she told him. "You said it yourself: It's a nursery rhyme."

Roshi's face was grave, and from his expression Goku and Bulma suddenly understood the seriousness of their situation.

"We must collect all seven Dragon Balls, then

recite this prayer to compel Shen Long, the Dragon, to appear." He closed his eyes as the words flowed. "Dragon, the test of seven has been fulfilled. I compel you to come forth and grant my wish."

Bulma was still stuck on her original idea that the Dragon Balls could be a source of endless energy. "Okay," she said to Roshi. "Did you just hear yourself? This is the twenty-second century!" She was outraged. "The Dragon Balls should be a source of power to run vacuum cleaners, not to bring a mythical creature to life."

Roshi turned to her. "It makes no sense unless you have the courage of faith."

Bulma rolled her eyes. She didn't want faith. She wanted to be famous for discovering an endless source of electric power.

Roshi said, "I have lived my life in your world questioning what I've learned from the ancient master. I have sacrificed and despaired because before tonight I could make no sense of it. But finally I can see."

"What makes you think it's happening now?" Goku asked.

Roshi stepped close to Goku and pointed one finger at the boy's chest. "You. You are the key somehow.

Gohan knew it. That's why he trained you."

Bulma was ready to move on. She'd had enough of the old man's mumbo-jumbo. Grabbing Goku's arm, she said, "Okay, Goku. You've found your Master Roshi. I've kept my part of the bargain. Now it's time you keep yours. Let's go."

Roshi stopped them from leaving. "If what Gohan says is true and Piccolo is here, this wish may be the only thing that can save our world."

Goku was caught between the promise he'd made to Bulma and his intuition that what Master Roshi was saying was true. There was only going to be one wish. What would it be?

For now, he decided that the most important thing was to find the Dragon Balls. He'd figure out the wish when all seven balls were in hand.

"We'll go," he told Bulma. "But we all go together."

Bulma attached a trailer to the speedster while Roshi threw food and gear into a net. Goku watched him pack. From the amount of stuff he was putting together, it looked to Goku like they were going on a long, long journey.

Roshi set the full net next to the speedster and

Goku came to help. He tied the ends of the package together and prepared to lift it into the small vehicle.

"The Shadow Crane Strike is the most basic of all the air bender techniques," Roshi told him, staying Goku's hand and preventing him from stashing the stuff on the bike.

Roshi took the bulging net back from Goku. He then balanced the pack on Goku's back, tying it into place with straps on Goku's shoulders.

"To learn what I have to teach you, you'll have to become stronger," he told Goku, as the boy strained under the weight of the pack. Goku grunted, but accepted that his new training had begun. He would learn what Roshi had to offer, even if it meant breaking his back. Literally.

Bulma laughed. "Goku looks like an ant carrying ten times his weight," she commented. She pointed at Roshi and told Goku, "You wanted him. Although I'm beginning to appreciate the entertainment value."

Bulma climbed onto the motorbike. Roshi got on behind her in Goku's regular seat.

"We will go to Stone Temple. It is a secret place where your grandfather Gohan and I were taught to master the energy of the three elements: air, fire, and water."

Roshi nodded. Bulma gunned the engine and the motorbike sped off down the road. Goku might have been resigned to his fate, but he wasn't happy about it. Fuming, he took off after them, the massive pack on his back, running as fast as he could.

# CHAPTER SEVEN

The motorbike sped along a narrow mountain path. Goku was amazed at how swiftly he could run with the pack strapped to his shoulders. That wasn't to say it was easy, it was just that he was surprised by his own strength and endurance.

By the time they reached the Stone Temple, Goku was still going, but was tired. A long break, maybe even a nap, would be good.

Finally, Goku caught up with Bulma and Roshi. He dumped the pack onto the motorbike's trailer and went over to join his friends.

Roshi explained why they were there. "The Stone Temple has been a source of solitude and enlightenment for millennia. Here you will learn what I learned from the ancient masters."

The three climbed to the top of a dune. The view was amazing! Before them stood eight giant stone pillars arranged in an asymmetrical pattern. The stones

stood guard over a desert that stretched endlessly before them. Even though there were no altars, the pillars
gave the area an aura of a sacred place.

Unfortunately, however, the mystical quality of the
place was diminished by the massive number of people
milling around. It looked like a tourist trap. No, on second glance, Goku realized the Stone Temple was being
used by groups of martial artists, all training on the
sacred ground.

"I thought you said this place was secret," Bulma
said to Roshi.

Roshi's jaw dropped. He couldn't believe how many
people were standing in the shadow of the ancient temple. "Unbelievable!" he exclaimed. "There's a snack
bar!"

Goku stepped forward. He had seen something unbelievable too.

"Is that Chi Chi?" he asked no one in particular.
Goku moved closer for a better look.

A group of martial artists sat in a large circle. Chi
Chi and another fighter were going at it in the center of
the group. Chi Chi unleashed a master combination of
spins and kicks, and easily dispatched the much heavier
and more muscular fighter.

Battle won, Chi Chi bowed to her sifu, her teacher,

and headed back to her place in the circle.

Goku intercepted her.

"Goku?" she exclaimed. "What are you doing here?"

"I was about to ask you the same thing," Goku replied.

Chi Chi looked down. She appeared to be embarrassed, as if confessing a personal secret.

"This is where everybody trains for the big tournament in Toi San," she told Goku. "That's what I wanted to tell you at the party. Before you suddenly took off."

Goku felt the need to apologize. "I'm sorry. I had personal reasons."

Chi Chi shook off his apology. "No. I heard about your grandfather's accident. I'm so sorry. The house collapsed?"

Goku wasn't ready to tell her what really happened. He shrugged. "Something like that," he said cryptically. "What did you want to tell me?"

"My deepest secret..." Chi Chi admitted. "I'm a fighter, too. Nobody else would understand."

At that, Goku shook his head in disbelief. He and Chi Chi had more in common than he possibly could have imagined.

He'd have liked to stay all day, talking to Chi Chi,

but Roshi's voice snapped him back to their quest.

"Goku!"

Turning, Goku saw Roshi beckoning him to their place on the dune.

"I gotta go," he told Chi Chi.

"Come to the tournament in Toi San," Chi Chi suggested. "Maybe we can find time to mix it up."

Man, that sounded good. Goku grinned at the thought of hanging out with Chi Chi in Toi San. He watched her walk back to her training group, then returned to where Bulma and Roshi were waiting.

"We can't train here," Roshi said with a shiver of repulsion. "My Ki is shriveling up as we speak."

"Hang on!" Bulma was looking at the now active DBE. "At least this won't be a total waste. I found a signal from another Dragon Ball!"

On the observation deck of Lord Piccolo's airship, Mai ran a hand through her hair. She had watched Goku and his friends arrive at the Stone Temple, observed Goku talk to Chi Chi, and then saw the group excitedly rush away from the martial arts training grounds.

It was time to report to Lord Piccolo.

Mai approached him with caution. Piccolo was quietly studying the Dragon Ball he had taken from the man in the jungle. He stared into it.

When he opened his palm, just a little bit, Mai could see that the Dragon Ball glowed hot red.

"My Lord," Mai began, but not until after Piccolo acknowledged her presence. "I have followed Muten-Roshi as directed. He is training a boy, Son Goku."

Piccolo looked at the Dragon Ball, still burning in his hand. His expression hardened.

"I could disrupt them," Mai suggested.

Piccolo shook his head. "No," he said. "Nothing will matter once I have all the Dragon Balls." Lord Piccolo was on a rampage to collect the powerful balls.

With a flip of his hand, the energy from the Dragon Ball shot out like a ray of light into the clouds. Lightning exploded across the heavens.

A few hours later, Lord Piccolo and Mai were standing at the side of a lake bed. Millions of gallons of water rose into the sky like rain falling upwards. Piccolo was draining the enormous lake with his powers, leaving only a soggy crater behind as the water disappeared.

Thousands of fish flopped and struggled for breath and life as only shallow pools of water and mud were left behind.

The Namekian and Mai walked to the middle of

the now empty lake bed. Reaching through a large pile of nearly dead fish, Lord Piccolo precisely grasped at the bottom of the lake. When he pulled his hand back, Mai saw that he was now holding the gleaming six-star Dragon Ball.

"Much easier to find without the water," Lord Piccolo commented, a grin stretched across his green, villainous face.

Goku was training nearby. He didn't know about Lord Piccolo, Mai, and the sixth Dragon Ball. What he did know was that if he moved, even the slightest bit, he'd plummet to his death.

"Now one hand!" Master Roshi called out to him.

Roshi and Bulma were riding the motorbike away from Stone Temple. Goku was in the trailer. Kind of. Actually, Goku was on the trailer, doing a handstand, as the bike zoomed along at fifty miles per hour.

He raised one hand, holding his balance steady.

"To master the second level of air bending you will have to control two things at once," Roshi explained to the upside-down Goku. Roshi held out an orange. "Now, knock this orange from my hand," he instructed.

Goku knew what the master meant. He took a deep breath and concentrated. His eyes blazed, locked onto the orange. Energy funneled through his body, gathering in the palm of his raised hand. Every muscle in his wrist tensed, and then with the slightest movement, Goku twisted his wrist, forcing the energy through his index finger toward the orange.

BLAM! The orange in Roshi's hand exploded. Orange juice and pulp plastered Roshi's face.

Suddenly the trailer rocked. Goku tumbled down, unable to balance on a single hand as the motorbike veered into the sand.

Goku wasn't hurt or else he would have yelled at Bulma. She'd veered off the road on purpose!

"I'm getting a strong signal from a Dragon Ball only three miles ahead," she told them, giddy with joy.

She twisted the throttle and the motorbike took off again, now across the sand. But it couldn't go far in the sand and the bike and trailer fantailed.

Next thing Bulma, Roshi, and Goku knew, the bike was out from under them. They were falling. Dropping straight down into a pit.

# CHAPTER EIGHT

Bulma, Goku, and Roshi leapt free of the bike as they plummeted thirty feet down into a large hole. They had fallen into a trap that was shaped like a gourd, the bottom wider than the top, with walls that curved inward.

Roshi grabbed Bulma as they fell, in a feeble attempt to cushion her from the impact of the ground. Goku smashed into the rounded wall, slicing right through the sand, causing a small avalanche of debris as he slammed into the hard soil.

He wasn't dead. That was good.

Goku pulled himself up, catching his breath. Bulma and Roshi were sitting up, too. The speedster was behind them, a twisted heap of metal pieces.

"What happened?" Bulma asked, her voice echoing off the sides of the pit.

"Need some help down there?" A face poked its head over the rim of the trap.

"Who are you?" Bulma called back. Goku could already see that the guy peering over at them was a few years older than he was. Maybe twenty or so.

"Yamcha," the guy replied.

Goku was about to say something, but Bulma cut in. "Let me handle this," she said to Goku, turning on the charm. "You're a real lifesaver, Yamcha," she yelled up. "We're stuck down here. I'll be soooo grateful if you can help me and my friends out."

It worked. Yamcha immediately held up a rope ladder. "For a pretty thing like you, no problem." He grinned at Bulma.

"Thank you," Bulma said. "You're a gentleman."

"I sure am," Yamcha laughed. "But I'm going to need some payment." He shined a flashlight down into the hole, surveying the situation. "Like...all your stuff."

Bulma was shocked. "Payment?"

Roshi shook his head at her. "Oh, Bulma." He sighed. "Who do you think made this trap?"

Yamcha shined his light on the motorbike. "Is that a capsule RX-550 roadster? Sweet."

Bulma was furious. "You're not a gentleman! You're nothing but a lowlife bandit."

"Yeah," Yamcha agreed. "But one with a rope

ladder. Think it over. 'Bout an hour after the sun comes out, it'll be over 120 degrees down there."

An hour later, Goku was about ten feet up the concave wall. His hand pressed into the sand, but with nothing firm to hold on to, the wall gave way and he fell to the ground. Again.

"Goku, take a break. The wall will be there after we eat." Roshi held out some food.

Goku looked back up at the wall as he stepped away. His prints were all over the cavern walls, reminders of all his previous attempts to climb out.

Reluctantly, Goku moved to the fire where Roshi and Bulma were heating food from Roshi's big pack. Roshi cut pieces of meat for them and served it on tin plates.

"Now all we need are marshmallows and a ghost story," Bulma joked, taking her plate and digging in.

Roshi took a few bites of his own meal, then said, "We have no marshmallows, but I do have a story."

Yamcha sat near his infra-red heater. A storm was brewing and the wind whipped around him. Undetected by his three captives, he settled near the pit's opening, eager to listen to Roshi's tale.

"Two thousand years ago, around 200 B.C.E., the earth was nearly destroyed," Roshi began. "It started with an eclipse by the blood moon. Fire rained from the sky, water covered the land, and storms raged everywhere. The only recorded history of this event came from China—the Qin Dynasty. They wrote of an invasion, not by men, but by gods from the sky." Roshi paused, setting down his plate before continuing. "They were called Nameks."

Roshi pushed his hand, his Ki, toward the fire. In the flames, images appeared. The images danced, free form, like a hallucination, never settling enough to form anything more than an impression.

Goku stared at the images before him. "Nameks." The memories came quickly. "They're the aliens my grandfather always talked about. He told me they discovered Earth by accident. Our two planets aligned during an eclipse."

Roshi pressed forward with the story. "Lord Piccolo and his right hand, a Saiyan called Oozaru the Destroyer, traveled to Earth hidden by meteors. They came to conquer the humans by destroying them all."

Goku looked more deeply into the fire. There he

witnessed glimpses of what he experienced when he touched a Dragon Ball. He could clearly see the red eyes and razor-sharp fangs of the demon that haunted him.

"Seven mystics banded together to fight the invaders," Roshi told them. "It was only through the courage of the ancient masters that Earth survived."

In the fire, Goku watched the scene unfold as a massive army of warriors were flattened by an energy wave thrown by Lord Piccolo.

"They sacrificed their lives to cast the Ma Fu Ba, a powerful curse that imprisoned Lord Piccolo into an encircling urn."

Goku saw the faces and hands of the masters as they cast the curse. Energy was released from their palms. A young Lord Piccolo was caught in a vortex of energy and sucked down into a prayer urn. Goku could practically hear Piccolo's screams as he disappeared.

"Before their deaths, the mystics created the Dragon Balls. So that their power, in the form of Shen Long the Dragon, might be used against a future enemy." Roshi sighed. "This story has been passed down through generations so that history will not repeat itself."

Bulma and Goku looked up at Roshi. Never had he looked more like the honorable master that he was, than in this moment.

"Lord Piccolo has somehow escaped," he told them with both certainty and concern. "In five days, the blood moon will eclipse the sun and bring forth Oozaru the Destroyer. Unless we find the Dragon Balls, we will have no defense against the onslaught."

"What a crock!" Yamcha's voice interrupted the end of Roshi's tale.

Everyone looked toward the top of the hole. "You expect me to believe that?" Yamcha asked.

Roshi responded immediately. "No. I do not. I think you are the kind of person who does not believe in anything because you have no faith."

Yamcha snorted. "Wrong, Grandpa. I believe in three things: me, myself, and I. That's all anyone can count on in this world."

Bulma was not impressed by Yamcha's declaration. "I feel sorry for you," she called up to him.

"Hey. I'm not the one stuck in a hole," Yamcha called back at her.

Bulma set her plate aside and stood up. She looked up at Yamcha and said, "Yes you are. You just don't know it. You may as well cover yourself in dirt because you're already dead inside."

From the expression on Yamcha's face, Goku could see that Bulma had hit Yamcha where it hurt.

"I don't know if I believe in his story," she told Yamcha. "But I believe in him."

Roshi gave Bulma a look to let her know he was impressed with how she was handling Yamcha.

Goku stood up. He'd had enough of Yamcha's teasing. "Let us out now!" Goku demanded. With a flying jump, Goku managed to soar twenty feet in the air.

Yamcha backed up in surprise. "Whoa there, jumping bean. One more outburst like that and I'm outta here."

Roshi was ready for a different tack. He moved over to their belongings. "We have no time to waste. Send down a net. You can pick up your payment."

"Now we're talkin'!" Yamcha smiled as he threw a cargo net over the side of the pit and waited for his booty.

When everything was packed into the cargo net, including the RX-550 capsule roadster, Yamcha set the engine of his truck to haul up the load. The net was heavy, almost too heavy for the truck, and the steel cable holding the net groaned under the strain.

Down in the pit, Bulma noticed that the signal for the Dragon Ball they'd been seeking was nearby. "The Dragon Ball is close," she told Goku and Roshi. "But I think it's buried underground."

Goku watched as all their possessions moved slowly toward the mouth of the pit. Losing them was bad. But finding another Dragon Ball was more important. "We'll need tools to excavate."

Even from the bottom of the pit, they could see that Yamcha's truck held every possible tool imaginable, including a large metal drill that was jutting out from the truck's frame.

Yamcha secured his payment, tying it off to the bed of his truck. He tossed a rope ladder down to Goku and said, "Nice doin' business with ya."

Roshi pulled himself up the ladder. "How would you like to make more money than you've ever dreamed of?" he asked Yamcha.

Yamcha delayed his departure. He was intrigued.

It wasn't but a few moments later that Bulma, Roshi, and Goku were standing by Yamcha's truck watching the large drill break through the cavern's sandy wall.

Bulma was nearby, but not too close. She was really mad. "You have no right to give away a third of the royalties of my invention," she told Roshi. "One day Dragon Balls could power the world."

"Don't worry," Roshi told her with a wink. "A third of zero is still zero."

With a slam and a crash, the drill broke through the wall.

"If that DBE thing is right," Yamcha pointed to the tracker in Bulma's hand. "The ball you're lookin' for is right here." He pulled the drill bit back, revealing a long, dark, sand-filled tunnel.

Goku was going in. As he moved to the tunnel's mouth, he had to pass Yamcha. "I guess if you hadn't robbed us we wouldn't be able to get this Dragon Ball," he said sarcastically.

"Everything happens for a reason," Yamcha replied with a shrug. At Bulma's impressed look, Yamcha explained, "Got that one from daytime TV."

Night had fallen by the time Goku retrieved the Dragon Ball from the tunnel. In the darkness, this ball's three stars shone their light just for him. The glow called to him and he reached for the ball as if drawn by a force greater than himself.

Goku wrapped his fingers around it. Visions flooded his head as he watched the frightful scene unfold within his eyes:

Red eyes glare. Razor sharp teeth flash. The demon slashes at bodies before him. His power is overwhelming. The bodies fall in quick succession. A closer look reveals that the bodies are Roshi, Bulma, and Yamcha. All dead.

Goku screamed. The screams kept coming until his throat was raw and hoarse.

"Goku," Roshi called him out of the vision. "It's all right, son."

Goku looked up at Roshi, dazed. With a shiver and a shake, he let the vision go. Once the world came back into clear focus, Goku dropped the Dragon Ball into his pouch and tightened the strings.

"What happened to you?" Yamcha wanted to know.

"You're in danger. Don't come any further with us," Goku told Yamcha.

"Right," Yamcha said, distrustful of Goku's warning. "I suppose the check's in the mail. I think I'll be keeping an eye on my investment."

He could not be talked out of it. Yamcha was now clearly a part of their team.

They had three Dragon Balls. Four more to go and their mission would be complete. But they had to find the balls before the eclipse.

# CHAPTER NINE

The airship sailed through the night sky, above the clouds. Mai was at the control panel in the laboratory. She was reviewing a seven-sided grid where a seven-sided glass "growth" chamber was illuminated from top to bottom.

Lord Piccolo now had three Dragon Balls too. To retrieve the remaining four, they were going to use a special sort of army.

"Your blood will give them life," Mai told him, indicating that he should sit in a chair specially made for him.

Lord Piccolo seated himself in the gleaming metal chair. Tubes led from the chair to the growth chamber. On the arms of the chair were cuffs. The cuffs were open, and inside each one, sharp needles lined the leather.

Piccolo placed his arms inside the cuffs and Mai closed the contraption via the control panel. They sealed with a mechanical hiss. Sharp needles were positioned to enter Piccolo's arms.

Mai walked quickly to the control panel. After keying several switches, the machine activated.

The needles pulled back, ready to strike.

Lord Piccolo, the Namek, tensed as the cuffs activated.

The bottom of the glass grid filled with Lord Piccolo's green essence. Blinding light and steam filled the room as the glass growth chambers became opaque. And inside the chamber, a dark form burst to life.

Mai looked pleased. "The Fu Lum is ready to serve you, my Lord." She released the cuffs and Lord Piccolo rose from the chair, recovering from the ordeal.

"The Dragon Balls are within my grasp and with them the future of man." His words were strong and clear. This time, he would not fail to bring about the destruction of man.

From within the glass, a fully formed Fu Lum Assassin snarled, scratching on the glass, begging for release. Lord Piccolo stepped closer, eager to inspect his new creation. It was fearsome.

Piccolo entered the growth chamber and moved behind the Fu Lum. He had one now. He wanted more. Lots more.

In a lightning swift move, Piccolo unsheathed a sword from his scabbard and struck downward, splitting the demon in half. Mai gasped in shock. The creature fell to the ground, then immediately regenerated its lost half.

Lord Piccolo laughed from the depths of his soul. One demon had now become two. The possibilities were endless.

With each passing hour, the moon moved nearer to the rising sun. The time of the eclipse was growing closer.

Bulma, Goku, Master Roshi, and Yamcha were traversing an abandoned road up the side of an active volcano. They'd been following the DBE, climbing all day, unsure what to expect when they reached the top.

Yamcha was carrying a pack laden with equipment. "Once we get the seven Dragon Balls," he asked, breathing heavily, "how soon can I expect to see some profit?"

Everyone ignored him.

"A month? A year?"

Bulma shifted her own pack on her back. She was carrying a number of holstered guns, prepared for trouble. Holding the DBE in one hand, she noted the red dot at the top of the volcano, then grumbled as the dot disappeared. Bulma shook the device and complained, "The high temps are screwing with the signal. I can't get a good read on it. I know we're close."

At the summit of the volcano, the four spread out, trying to locate the Dragon Ball that they knew was close by. Steam rose through vents in the volcanic rock. Lava bubbled from beneath the surface. The air rippled from the heat.

They were all sweaty and exhausted, except for Goku. He was physically prepared for this challenge, but mentally? He wasn't feeling very confident.

Yamcha climbed onto a small outcropping of pumice. Using the higher vantage point to look around, he surveyed the area through a pair of binoculars. From beneath him a steam vent suddenly erupted.

"Owww!" Yamcha jumped high in the air, grabbing his butt. "Hey!" he called to the others. "I just got fried..." He paused, then delivered the good news. "... But I can see it!"

Yamcha pointed to a mini crater nearby. He was right. A tiny dot sat near the crater. It was a Dragon Ball. Unfortunately, to get there, someone was going to have to figure out how to cross a lake of molten lava.

Yamcha climbed back down to the others. He stated the obvious. "The problem is how to get across."

While Bulma and Yamcha heatedly discussed the engineering issues, Roshi looked at Goku. Ever since his last vision in the sand cave, Goku hadn't been the same. He'd been quiet and withdrawn.

Goku turned to the old man. "Master Roshi, the Dragon Balls..."

"They've been speaking to you." Roshi finished Goku's thought. "They are showing you a future."

Fear, so strong he could nearly taste it, rose within Goku. He whispered, "There's a demon with red eyes and razor-sharp claws."

"Oozaru the Destroyer,"said Roshi, identifying the demon.

But the old man didn't need to. Goku already thought he knew what he was seeing.

"He will kill you and Bulma and Yamcha." Goku confessed the truth of what he'd seen. The truth that had been weighing him down.

Master Roshi reacted only slightly. "This is a dark warning," he admitted.

"I need to defeat Oozaru." It was as much a statement as a question of how.

Roshi nodded, considering. "Goku, understand that

the future is always changing. Pay attention and let the dragon show you its lessons."

Goku was not sure what Roshi meant, but it lightened his spirit slightly. He would take the master's words to heart and see what he could learn.

Goku and his friends were preparing to cross the lava river. Their supplies were packed. They were motivated. The only issue remaining was how they were going to do it.

Bulma stated the obvious problem one last time. "The temperature of the lava is around one thousand two hundred degrees. We have nothing that can withstand the heat long enough for you to get across," she told Goku.

"I know some guys who know some guys who can 'borrow' a helicopter," Yamcha suggested.

Before Bulma could respond to Yamcha's nonsense, Mai stepped out from behind a craggy formation of pumice stone. A jet pack was strapped to her back.

Bulma immediately recognized her. "She's the one who stole my Dragon Ball," she shouted, pointing a finger at Mai.

From her holster, Mai quickly pulled out a slick semi-automatic pistol. She fired. Goku and Roshi hit the ground. Yamcha and Bulma dove for cover.

Mai ignited her jet pack and launched herself. There was no doubt in anyone's mind. She was going after their Dragon Ball, and whereas they had nothing, she had the means to reach it.

Goku would have rushed after her, figuring out what to do as he went along, but from seemingly nowhere, four Fu Lum Assassins sprung into the air. The team was under attack!

Each evil warrior had four long, sharp blades tucked behind them, like a fan of feathers from a bird of prey.

Roshi moved into combat position first. He threw a sword into the air toward Goku just as the Fu Lum Assassins landed in an arc around the boy.

Goku and Roshi began to battle the four Fu Lum.

Bulma and Yamcha ran after Mai into the lava field. They still had no plan, but they knew they had to stop her. They would find a way.

Goku struck out with rage. His blade flashed, slicing through two of the assassins. Two down, two to go, he thought to himself, feeling like this was going to be easier than he first expected. The Fu Lum hadn't even had time to unsheathe their weapons. They fell to the earth, unmoving.

Roshi fought the other two warriors. Goku, feeling confident, came to help, his blade flashing, ready to take them down in two more quick slashes.

Roshi suddenly blocked Goku's blade with his own. Goku glanced at Roshi angrily. He didn't know why Roshi would put them both in danger. He could have killed the two remaining Fu Lum. It would have been over.

"It's not always wise to strike first." Roshi directed Goku's attention to the first assassins that Goku had sliced in two. "You have put us in grave danger," Roshi told Goku as he continued to watch the two "dead" warriors.

"Danger?" Goku asked with a huff. "I've saved us."

Goku followed Roshi's gaze. The two fallen assassins were regenerating into four distinct creatures.

All around them, six Fu Lum Assassins assumed their fighting stance. Two of the Fu Lums were perfectly formed. Two others were mostly formed. One had split arms and the other, a head growing out from its shoulder. The last two were completely deformed. One had a perfect upper body with crab-like legs. The other had perfect legs with a spindly praying mantis body.

Goku and Roshi stepped back. Now they were vastly outnumbered.

"They are called regenerators," Roshi told Goku. "My master taught me about this Namekian trick. We cannot draw blood or dismember any part of their bodies."

Goku realized what he had done. It was true, he'd acted impulsively. "Did your master tell you how we're supposed to fight them?" he asked.

Roshi looked like he was searching his memory for the answer. "That might be a problem," he admitted.

The assassins lashed out. Goku and Roshi were good fighters and blocked blades with their swords, but could make no offensive counterattack.

"We're in trouble here," Goku breathed. "What do we do?"

In the second between attacks, Roshi shrugged. "My mind's a blank. I must have ditched my lessons that day."

For the moment, Goku could only focus on staying alive. He spun, jumping and blocking six blades as they flashed down upon him. Roshi blocked the onslaught from one of the other assassins, his hands moving at the speed of light.

"All work and no play makes Roshi a dull boy," he commented casually. At this point, humor was just about all they had left.

In the lava field, Bulma dashed forward, trying to get a clean shot at Mai with her laser gun. Suddenly she saw Mai above them. Without any hesitation, Bulma fired.

Direct hit! Mai's jet pack smoked and sputtered as the bullet slammed through it. Mai plummeted down onto the lava field.

Bulma and Yamcha ran toward where Mai had fallen. They could see her now hurrying over sharp rocks and bizarre volcanic formations, but then she seemed to disappear into the landscape.

On guard, Bulma approached a fairly large outcrop of rocks, just the right size and shape to make a good hiding place. She readied her weapon.

Nearby, Yamcha shouted out, "I found her pack."

Yamcha's voice distracted Bulma, only for a split second, but just long enough for Mai to reach through the cracks of a hardened lava wall and snag Bulma's weapon out of her hand. Before surrendering the gun, Bulma fired, but the weapon discharged harmlessly.

Mai broke Bulma's grip on her gun. The weapon dropped out of reach.

Mai came out from the safety of the lava wall and began her attack on Bulma in earnest. She snapped

Bulma's head back with a high kick and then began beating her with a series of roundhouse kicks. Unable to defend herself, Bulma collapsed to the ground.

Yamcha came to Bulma's rescue, tackling Mai and crushing her against the sharp lava wall. The battle was vicious. Yamcha and Mai were evenly matched. The fighting went on until, at last, Yamcha attacked Mai with a concentrated burst of power. He tackled her to the ground.

Mai struggled, until suddenly, she pressed a button on her bright red suit. Electricity arcs from metal nodes slammed through Yamcha. The shock and force threw him off. His head hit a sharp lava outcrop and Yamcha fell still.

Bulma retrieved her gun and leveled it at Mai, blasting her with bullets. Mai rolled away, the bullets ricocheting off the rocks all around. Fleeing into the safety of the lava field, Mai disappeared from view.

# CHAPTER TEN

Goku and Roshi were pinned against a lake of lava and volcanic fire as the Fu Lum Assassins pursued them relentlessly. Roshi disarmed an assassin, then ducked an attack. He kicked one of the attackers against another deformed assassin. The deformed Fu Lum was knocked off balance and tumbled into the lake of fire.

Screaming, the deformed Fu Lum sunk down into the molten rock. The hot liquid quickly covered him, and bubbles arose in the lava as the assassin died.

"Goku!" Roshi shouted to his disciple who was fighting other Fu Lum nearby. "Into the lava! That's the only way to stop them!"

Goku was immediately energized by Master Roshi's solution to the Fu Lum problem. Leaping, spinning, kicking, punching, he became a vortex of action as he drove the crooked-headed Fu Lum into the lake.

But he didn't have a chance to relish in his victory. As he turned back, another Fu Lum thrust its blade toward

Goku's head.

Using a classic martial arts maneuver, Goku clapped his hands together, effectively stopping the blade a mere inch from his eyes. Goku twisted his hands, turning the assassin toward the lake of fire, and tossed him into the boiling lava.

From the corner of his eye, Goku could see Roshi was having trouble. The old man had fallen, having had his legs taken out from under him by the crab-like Fu Lum. Roshi slammed to the ground and the assassin was swinging his powerful arms, pummeling the master.

Goku couldn't reach Roshi to help. The spindly Fu Lum was attacking and Goku quickly discovered that its long arms made it an unusual adversary. Goku was pushed back into the craggy rocks before he grabbed the Fu Lum in an amazing move and sent the monster soaring into the lava.

The lake of fire was now littered with Fu Lum Assassins. Oddly, though, their alien bodies didn't disintegrate from the heat of the lava. Instead, they floated like stepping stones across the molten lake.

On his own, Roshi finally managed to get the upper hand on the crab-like Fu Lum. He sent the monster soaring toward the lake. A split second before the Fu Lum met his doom, Goku dove forward, saving the Fu Lum from certain death. Roshi was now the one confused. That was the last of the Fu Lum warriors.

He turned to Goku as the boy pulled out his sword.

"What are you doing?!" Roshi demanded to know.

"We have to make more." Goku struck rapidly, cutting the crab-like Fu Lum into four pieces. Roshi moved to stop him, but it was too late. Four more Fu Lum began to regenerate.

Goku grabbed one of the new Fu Lum with a blinding-quick move. He tossed the assassin into the lava toward the crater, where the Dragon Ball was still waiting. The assassin died from the heat, but became another stepping stone in the lava lake.

"That's how we get across," Goku told Roshi, showing him how the alien bodies floated on the lava surface.

Goku continued to make new Fu Lum warriors. As each Fu Lum began to regenerate, sprouting different appendages, Goku chucked them into the lake.

One more. That was all they needed. The final Fu Lum had grown arms and legs by the time Goku sent it flying into the lava. Right before it splashed down, the Fu Lum sprouted a head just in time to see that it was about to plunge into the molten lake.

The dead Fu Lum Assassins formed a perfect path across the lake of fire leading right to the Dragon Ball prize.

Goku looked at Roshi, confirming that this was the only way to get the Dragon Ball. Goku would go alone. With one final glance at the old man Goku took a running start and jumped onto the first of the floating Fu Lum.

His strength and agility were astounding as he hopped, skipped, and jumped toward the mini crater. At times Goku was going so fast it looked as if he were flying. Closer and closer he came to the crater. At the lip of the crevasse, he reached up, grabbing onto the sharp rocks. His hands were cut by the jagged edges of the lava stone, and he struggled. Hanging thirty feet above the molten lake, Goku managed to pull himself up into the crater.

The six stars of the Dragon Ball called to him. The stars' light grabbed hold of Goku and refused to let him go. He reached out for the ball, and there was almost a spark of brilliance from the stars as he made contact. The vision began:

The monstrous red eyes open. The flash of razor sharp fangs. An image of Roshi, Bulma, and Yamcha lying dead.

And then, more. Goku leaps. Oozaru attacks. His movements are a blur. Power punches. Leg whips. Elbow smashes. A leaping side kick.

Every move is anticipated by Oozaru, blocking, then countering with such power that Goku is crushed against his fist.

The vision faded, incomplete, leaving Goku wondering about his fate. And what happened to Oozaru the Destroyer.

Exhausted, Goku dropped to his knees, still at the top of the crater.

"Goku!" Roshi shouted out to him. "Come back!" Goku raised his head and looked around. The heat was beginning to take a toll on the Fu Lum's bodies and some were submerging into the lake of fire.

Goku jumped down and began crossing back to the other shore. He stepped on the backs of the Fu Lum, hopping across the lava. Landing solidly on a face-up Fu Lum, Goku could see Roshi waiting for him in the near distance, safely on the opposite shore.

Pop! With its last gasp of breath, the upturned Fu Lum reached its horrible arm out of the burning brew and grabbed Goku's leg. Hard as he tried, Goku couldn't shake the Fu Lum's grasp. The assassin was sinking, pulling Goku down into the molten lava with him.

With the reflexes of a true master artist, Roshi was on the move. He reached for Gohan's bow staff.

"Nyoibo extend!" The bow staff shot out, striking the Fu Lum and dislodging its grasp on Goku.

Goku finished the last steps and finally made it back to

All of Goku's training thus far had led to this moment. The battle was beginning. It was him against his master. Goku didn't like to lose!

# "Stay focused!"

## "Name's Goku."

Within an instant, Goku was moving at a speed faster than either bully could attack. His body blurred as he jumped, initiating a back flip.

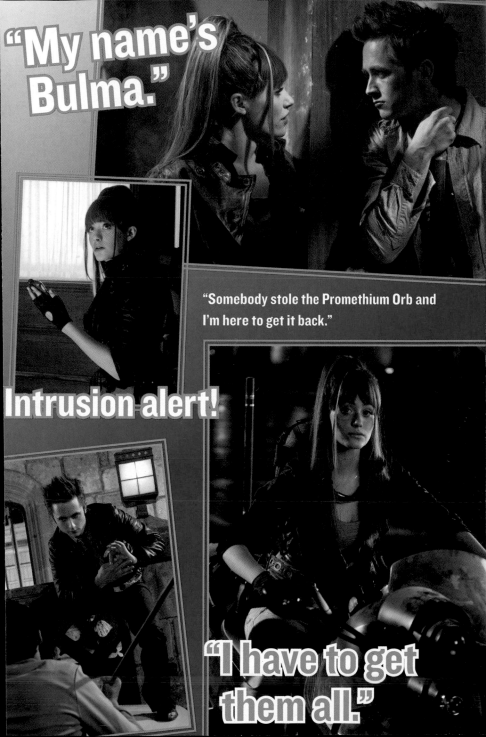

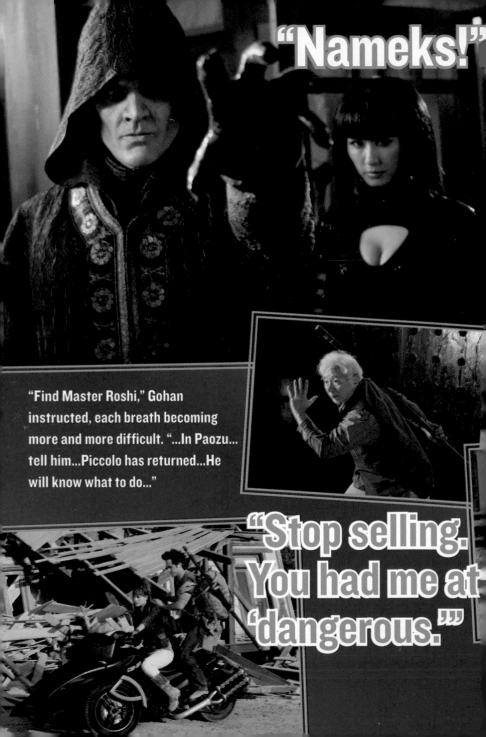

**"Nameks!"**

"Find Master Roshi," Gohan instructed, each breath becoming more and more difficult. "...In Paozu... tell him...Piccolo has returned...He will know what to do..."

**"Stop selling. You had me at 'dangerous.'"**

"Seven Dragon Balls must be found
For all men's fate will be bound
To battle forces of death and fear
And compel Shen Long to appear..."

"You might need back-up."

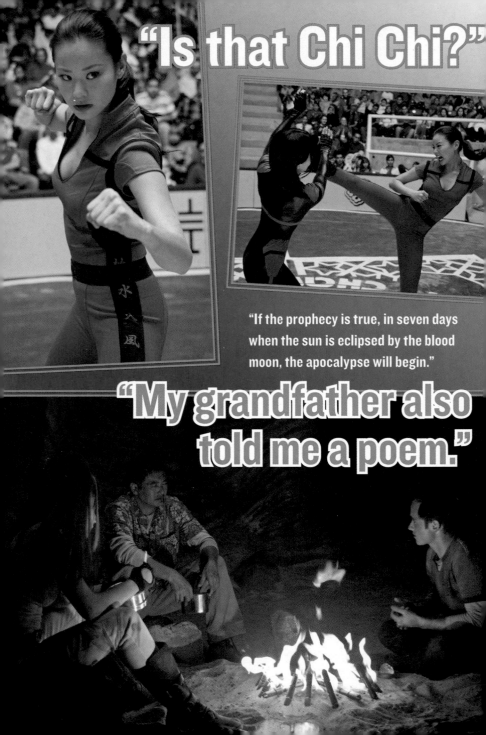

"A third of zero is still zero."

He could not be talked out of it. Yamcha was now clearly a part of their team.

# "Who are you?"

Tumbling through the blazing inferno, Goku was stunned by what he saw: two Chi Chis, identical in every way, were before him, engaged in battle.

shore, tired and mentally drained. He'd battled the Fu Lum, run across a lava lake, found the Dragon Ball, endured its vision, and nearly died on his way back. Now, when he had nothing left to give, Yamcha was shouting at him.

"Okay." Yamcha approached Goku angrily. "First of all, nobody said anything about guns." He touched his head, and when he pulled back his hand it was covered with blood. "I mean, this is blood here. And what were those things, the guys that split in half and became whole again?"

"They are Nameks," Roshi calmly explained. "Called regenerators. Created from Lord Piccolo himself."

Yamcha pressed the sore spot on his head again. He was trying desperately to accept the truth. To take it all in. "All that stuff about aliens and the invasion...that's all true?"

Roshi nodded.

"Wow." Yamcha was no longer angry. He looked surprised and confused and like his head hurt, both from the injury and the reality of his situation.

"The eclipse is in two days. We'll never find the other Dragon Balls in time," Bulma sighed.

Roshi agreed. Their time to retrieve all the Dragon Balls and save Earth was running out. "The only chance the world has now is in Toi San."

# CHAPTER ELEVEN

The Toi San Tournament of Champions had already begun.

A match was raging on the main stage. Goku watched as Chi Chi threw wickedly quick combinations of kicks at an obviously overmatched opponent. Chi Chi's leg whipped out, catching her hooded opponent in the head. Chi Chi moved in for the final blow but the opponent managed to sneak in a slash while blocking Chi Chi's onslaught.

Chi Chi was bleeding, but the contest wasn't quite over. Although Chi Chi was well positioned to win, her opponent decided to quit and forfeit the remainder of the match. She simply stepped back, out of bounds.

The judge entered the ring and called an end to the fight. Chi Chi had a confused look on her face as her opponent walked away.

"Why enter the tournament if you don't want to fight?" Chi Chi called after the hooded figure.

As the judge raised Chi Chi's arm in victory, blood dripped from the cut on her forearm.

In the nearby shadows, hidden from Chi Chi and the rest of the tournament, Mai removed her hood. She got what she came for. In a small vial, she held a few drops of Chi Chi's blood. Blood she gathered when she slashed Chi Chi's arm during the fight. After that, Mai had no reason to continue fighting. Chi Chi might have won the fight, but Mai looked at the small vial of blood and felt equally victorious.

Goku rushed up to Chi Chi as she came down the stage steps.

"Great match," he told her excitedly.

"Goku!" When Chi Chi saw him, her face lit up. "You came." She ran over and gave him an affectionate hug. The emotion of the embrace caught them both by surprise. She was flushed pink, obviously embarrassed, when she pulled away. Chi Chi smiled, but Goku was beaming.

"Are you in the tournament?" she asked.

"No," he replied, glancing around at the stage and the crowd. "I'm here for something else."

Chi Chi, having regained her composure, turned on

the charm. "Something more important than me?"

Goku brought his gaze back to her. "Actually you're one of the reasons why it's so important."

From her expression, Goku could tell that she didn't quite understand what he meant, but he wasn't ready to explain to her about the Dragon Balls and the eclipse and Lord Piccolo. He'd tell her eventually. But for now, he wanted to simply enjoy the time they had together.

She took his arm in hers and the two of them walked off into the tournament fairgrounds.

A silver-haired monk was meditating in an alcove at the Toi San Temple. He was so focused on his work that he had effectively tuned out the noise and chaos of the competitions around him.

He slowly sifted sand through his fingers, creating an elaborate and colorful pattern. The sand spread deliberately to reveal a beautiful Tibetan Mandela in the pattern of a mystic circle design called a cosmogram.

The door to the temple opened and a gust of wind swept across his design, altering the pattern.

The monk looked up to find Roshi walking toward him.

"Sifu Norris," Roshi greeted the ancient monk.

"How is my favorite skeptic?" Sifu Norris responded,

lowering his eyes back to the Mandela. "Are you here to discuss our wasted lives, or have you found another way to profit from our training?" There was a bitterness in the monk's voice that Roshi had fully expected.

"I've come to apologize, Sifu Norris," he said with a small bow. "Everything I've questioned before I now know is all true."

Sifu Norris raised his head to look directly at Roshi. "Nameks?" he barely breathed the word.

Roshi nodded. "Have returned."

"The prophecy?" the monk questioned.

Roshi nodded again. "The blood moon will eclipse the sun tomorrow, bringing forth the Saiyan, Oozaru the Destroyer."

Sifu Norris's face showed surprise. "That means Lord Piccolo has escaped from his containment."

"He is here," Roshi responded simply.

Sifu Norris was quiet for a moment, considering. "Somehow I thought being proven right would feel better."

Roshi gave his old friend a smile. "I need your help," Roshi told him. "I need another containment vessel."

"The Ma Fu Ba. The energy of the elements. Air, fire, and water. That's how you'll defeat Lord Piccolo," Sifu Norris instructed. "It's also how you'll die. The Ma

Fu Ba will consume all your life forces."

Roshi gave a wry half smile. All this, he already knew. "When you put it that way, the plan sucks. But you and I know it's the only way. I'm the only one who can do it."

Sifu Norris looked compassionately at his old friend. He reached out, then closed his hand into a fist. Roshi repeated the movement. It was a symbol of strength and camaraderie.

"I'll have it ready by morning." Sifu Norris took one last long look at Roshi, then lowered his gaze back to the cosmogram he'd been creating.

That evening, Bulma was sitting on a concrete stoop in front of a Chinese barbecue. The window was filled with roasted ducks. Dead ducks. She mused at the irony. She was feeling very sympathetic. She now believed that she was going to share the same fate. Yamcha too. And Roshi and Goku. They were all "dead ducks."

Yamcha approached, carrying two cups. He sat next to her as they glumly sipped their drinks.

"I wanted to be famous," Bulma said sadly.

"I wanted to be rich," Yamcha put in.

Bulma sighed. "It looks like neither one of us are going to get what we wanted."

Bulma scanned the marketplace. People were going about their ordinary lives. The butcher behind her chopped the neck off a cooked duck. Bulma shuddered.

"Look at these people, they have no idea." Part of her wanted to shout out about Lord Piccolo, the eclipse, and the destruction that was going to come the next day.

"Maybe it's better not to know," Yamcha said, pausing to sip his drink. "They still have their dreams."

Bulma looked at Yamcha over the rim of her cup. There was something good in him. She hadn't noticed it before. But now…"I never thought I could enjoy talking to a thief," she remarked with a wink.

"Well, I've always had a thing for brainiacs, especially ones who can handle a gun," Yamcha teased back. "Besides, I'm not so bad once you get to know me."

Bulma raised her eyebrows and flirted, "Maybe I like bad men."

Yamcha couldn't contain his surprise. "Good to know on the day before the end of the world."

Bulma turned away, a little embarrassed that she just sort of admitted that she liked Yamcha. Suddenly a thought occurred to her. "Wait a second, we have four

Dragon Balls."

Yamcha knew exactly where she was going. "Piccolo needs all seven or else he's not going to be able to make his wish either."

A grin spread across Bulma's face. "Hey, there's still a chance for you to make your thirty percent."

"You mean thirty-three and a third!" Yamcha corrected with a grin of his own.

In the Toi San Temple courtyard, Roshi was practicing his art. He moved with grace and fluidity. Goku was with him, following his every move. There was little time left in the night and Goku wanted to learn as much as he could. He had to be ready for whatever it was that dawn would bring.

Goku copied his master step by step, trying to find the perfect balance. The form was synchronized movement, one position flowing gently into the next.

The two moved in silhouette. Their movements were graceful and poetic.

When Roshi finished, he addressed Goku. "The final level of the air bender technique is the Kamehame-ha."

Goku stepped closer to Roshi. "Grandfather told me about this move. He said I wasn't ready to learn it."

"You're not," Roshi agreed. "But time is running out. To master the Kame-hame-ha you have to master your Ki." Roshi brought his hands to his chest. "Draw on the power of the universe. Channel it through you. Focus it."

In Roshi's hands, a ball of blue energy ignited. Goku noticed that Roshi's energy was more fluid than his own. Goku wished that his was smooth, but the few times he'd been able to channel his Ki, it was rough and tumble, shaky and uneven.

Roshi held his energy in control, then said, "Release." The ball flew out and in a flash, set a torch in the courtyard aflame. "The more you put yourself into the Kame-hame-ha, the greater the power."

It was Goku's turn. He concentrated, pulling his hands to his chest as Roshi had done. A small blue ball of energy ignited! Surprised, Goku shifted his hands. The slight movement caused the ball to disappear.

"Practice," Roshi instructed Goku. "Light the torches in the courtyard." Roshi turned to go. "I'll see you in the morning."

Sifu Norris, along with Roshi and seven other monks, sat in a circle. In the center rested a ceramic pot with a lid hanging off the side.

The monks chanted. There was a fervor in their voices that matched the power of the melody. Each individual monk took a turn offering a prayer. The monks passed their hands over the ceramic pot as they sent some of their own strength into the clay.

With each prayer, the inside of the pot grew blacker.

It was Roshi's turn to offer his prayer. He gathered his energy for the task and passed his hands over the pot...

Goku had been working the torches all night. He was tired. The only torch that was on fire was the one Roshi had lit earlier. Goku's use of the Kame-hame-ha was having no effect. The energy balls either dissipated into smoke or missed the torches wildly when he sent them out.

Frustrated, he pulled a torch from the ground and began to light it with the torch that was already burning. At least then, two torches would glow. Instead of the one that continually mocked him.

"That's cheating."

Goku turned to discover Chi Chi dropping down from the temple wall, moving toward him. As she jumped down, Goku could see the small scar on her arm from the day's fight.

"You're supposed to light the torches with your Ki," she told him, as if he didn't already know.

Goku sighed. "You've been watching me?"

Chi Chi nodded and pointed up to the rooftop where she'd been sitting in the shadows.

"Then you know why I have to cheat."

Chi Chi laughed.

"My grandfather said to master my Ki. I have to be at one with myself and my enemy. I still don't understand what that means." Goku scratched his forehead. He was exhausted from trying so hard.

"Maybe you need an incentive," Chi Chi suggested.

Goku gave her a questioning look.

"There are five torches in the courtyard. I'm five paces away from you. Every time you light a torch, you get to move one step closer to me." Chi Chi coyly smiled.

Goku felt his heart flip in his chest. The challenge was intriguing. He was certainly willing to try. Pulling his hands back, his energy gathered and the blue ball ignited. Goku exhaled with renewed focus, sending it out toward a torch.

The torch lit!

Goku smiled and took a step closer to Chi Chi. She nodded in encouragement, praise in her eyes.

Again, he pulled his hands back, formed the ball and sent it out. Another torch caught fire!

Goku took another step toward the girl. Pulling his hands back a third time, he lit the energy ball and sent it out. This time, he missed.

"Only three more." Chi Chi encouraged him. "Concentrate."

Goku was feeling a little frazzled. He tried again. And missed again.

"Take one step back," Chi Chi said.

"That wasn't the rule," Goku protested.

"My game, my rules." Chi Chi was strict. And Goku stepped back.

Goku went to try again. He pulled his hands back, this time noticing that there was something uncomfortable with the way he was holding his hands.

"It doesn't feel right," he said. "I must be missing something."

"Goku. You have to make every move your own." Chi Chi shared her experience.

He considered her advice. This time he brought back his hands not to his chest as Master Roshi had shown him but to the right side, by his waist. The new position forced him to turn his hips, coiling his body. When the energy ball ignited now, it was brighter and more powerful than ever.

Using all his strength, Goku sent it sailing. Every torch in the courtyard immediately flamed.

He'd done it. Goku had mastered his Ki and performed the Kame-hame-ha.

With large steps, he covered the remaining distance to Chi Chi and hugged her tightly. They both savored his success, momentarily unaware of the almost full moon filling the sky with an eerie cold blue glow.

# CHAPTER TWELVE

Bulma was asleep in the ancient temple's sleeping quarters. The accommodations were sparser than she was used to. But a simple mat for a bed and rough-spun cotton blankets didn't prevent her from falling asleep.

A noise in the hall caused Bulma to open her eyes. She leapt up from her bed and hurried over to the door.

In the hallway, she saw a darkened figure emerging from Goku's room.

Ever on the alert, Bulma armed herself with a weapon and within seconds had it trained on the figure.

"Stop right there," Bulma demanded.

The figure turned. It was Chi Chi.

"I'm sorry. I didn't mean to wake anybody," Chi Chi said, holding her hands behind her back.

"No, I'm sorry," Bulma replied, lowering her gun. "Go back to what you were doing."

"I was just leaving," Chi Chi said.

Just then, Yamcha came out of the next room. "What's going on here?" he asked the girls.

"Nothing," they both responded at the exact same time.

Yamcha yawned. "Isn't there a curfew in the temple?" He turned to go back into his own room.

"Good night," Chi Chi said politely, walking away a little too quickly.

The hairs on Bulma's neck rose as she watched Chi Chi turn the corner. Something didn't feel right.

Not a second later Goku came down the hall from the other direction. "You guys are up late," he said.

Yamcha immediately noticed that Goku wasn't coming from his own room. "You weren't in your room?"

Bulma looked from one boy to the other, then whipped out the DBE. It indicated four dots moving away from them.

As fast as she could, Bulma headed after Chi Chi. "She has the Dragon Balls!" Bulma shouted back at the boys.

Goku and Yamcha were hard on her heels.

Chi Chi sprinted down the labyrinth of the temple hallways. Bulma, Goku, and Yamcha were in hot pursuit.

Chi Chi stopped long enough to raise an alien-looking weapon, pointing it straight at them.

As Bulma turned the corner, Chi Chi fired. A ray of energy blasted toward Bulma. Reacting like lightning, Goku tossed Bulma to the ground in the same moment the temple hallway exploded. Chi Chi fired several more volleys and a gigantic fireball consumed the walkway.

Chi Chi ran into the courtyard. She began to smile when she realized that Goku and his friends were no longer behind her.

From seemingly nowhere, a powerful kick knocked her to the ground. Chi Chi's weapon clattered away.

Chi Chi looked up to find...Chi Chi standing over her.

"Who are you?" the real Chi Chi asked.

The Chi Chi on the ground got up. She was dressed almost identically to the other Chi Chi. They squared off and the two Chi Chis began to fight.

Goku yanked Bulma and Yamcha back from the fire.

"Find another way," he told them, motioning for them to go back. Goku then took a running leap and jumped through the flames.

Tumbling through the blazing inferno, Goku was

stunned by what he saw: two Chi Chis, identical in every way, were before him, engaged in battle. Roundhouse kicks were followed by powerful punches. Finally a powerful kick connected and one Chi Chi fell to the ground, dazed.

As the standing Chi Chi moved to finish the other one off, the Chi Chi lying on the ground looked toward Goku. "Help me," she pleaded.

Goku sprang into action with a flurry of kicks and punches, battling Chi Chi. She worked to block his fearsome fight.

Quietly, the Chi Chi on the ground picked herself up. While safely guarding the pouch of Dragon Balls hidden in her one hand, she picked up her alien weapon.

Goku, meanwhile, broke through Chi Chi's amazing skill, knocking her not just down to the ground, but unconscious as well. Standing over his victim, Goku noticed the scar on her arm that she'd sustained the previous day when she was scratched in the tournament.

Goku was mad at himself. He was too impulsive sometimes.

Turning slowly, Goku knew he was in trouble.

"Wrong one," evil Chi Chi mocked him. She fired so quickly that Goku barely had time to raise his hands as the blast hit him point blank.

Goku was slammed to the ground.

Bulma and Yamcha, along with Roshi and a few other monks, came out of the temple in time to see Chi Chi transforming. Within seconds, she had reverted back to her true form: Mai. Dragon Balls safely in her possession, Mai took off. She headed toward a bluff and dove off the edge. Not a second later, a high-tech helicopter rose from below and swerved away. Mai was swinging from an attached rope ladder. She had escaped and taken the Dragon Balls with her.

The monks fought to control the blaze in the temple while Roshi hurried over to Goku's side. The boy's skin was alabaster, his eyes open but unseeing. Roshi tried to revive the boy, but nothing he did seemed to have any effect.

"He's alive but barely," Roshi said, holding one hand gently to Goku's temple.

Bulma moved to check on Chi Chi, who stirred, but remained completely knocked out. "She's going to be fine," Bulma reported.

Roshi was glad, he needed to give all his energy to Goku, not split it among the two. He rocked back, sitting on his heels, and closed his eyes in concentration. A powerful breath filled Roshi's body with light. Blood rushed into his arms, making him seem much larger than his own size. Then Roshi reached his hands to the heavens.

A ball of blue energy formed between Roshi's hands. He gathered it toward his chest and pushed the energy into the boy.

"Grandfather, I'm so happy to see you." Goku embraced his grandfather tightly. "Are you here for me?"

Gohan pushed the boy away, stepping back. "It's not your time, Goku. There is much left to do."

Goku lowered his head in shame. "I can't. The Dragon Balls have shown me. I can't defeat Oozaru."

"Always have faith in who you are," Gohan told Goku and then slowly disappeared.

"Kame-hame-ha!" Roshi shouted to the sky, driving his own energy hard and fast into Goku's weakened body. The energy coursed through the boy's veins, invading every cell. Goku was suddenly racked with spasms. His body moved entirely on its own, out of control. Goku screamed as he returned to consciousness.

Next to him, Roshi fell back, completely depleted.

He had spent much of his life force saving the life before him.

"Pain is good," Roshi told Goku as the boy opened his eyes. Only it was unclear if he was talking about Goku's pain or his own.

As Goku sat up, catching his breath and regaining his strength, Bulma pulled out the DBE. She could see the dots all coming together.

"We're too late," Bulma reported. "They have all seven Dragon Balls."

Everyone was stunned. They needed a plan. Immediately.

The sky above them began to brighten with the dawning of the dreaded day of the eclipse.

"Dragon Temple," Roshi told them. "That's where he'll resurrect Shen Long. We have to get there before the eclipse."

Yamcha would drive his utility truck with the entire crew riding in it. Goku, Bulma, and Roshi all rushed to jump in. In the nick of time, Sifu Norris ran out of Toi San Temple, stopping them from hurrying off too soon. He was carrying the containment vessel.

The old master was clearly exhausted, having worked with the monks all night. He handed the ceramic pot to Roshi.

"The enchantments are strong," Roshi declared, cradling the pot safely in his hands.

"Pray they are enough to contain Piccolo," Sifu Norris replied. "Good luck, my friend. We will meet again on the other side."

Roshi nodded.

They were ready.

"Where am I going?" Yamcha asked Roshi. He pressed the gas pedal to the floor.

Roshi indicated a steep mountain pass. "Dragon Temple is hidden down in the plains below us."

Bulma noticed Piccolo's airship floating overhead and pointed it out to the others. It hovered over a large, open field. "We'll never make it. Not before the sunrise," she said, defeated.

"Hang on," Yamcha told her, "This baby's still got a few tricks up its sleeves." He skidded the truck to a stop, then steered directly toward the edge of a thousand foot cliff.

"What are you doing?" Bulma shouted, panicked. "I hope you're not trying to impress me."

Yamcha stomped on the accelerator. The truck lurched forward.

"I wouldn't mind, but I'll settle for scaring you." He laughed as he launched the truck over the side of the cliff.

# CHAPTER THIRTEEN

Bulma's scream could be heard the whole thousand feet down the cliff. Yamcha pulled a few levers as the truck got closer and closer to the ground below. Suddenly, the tires folded under and a bright flash of ignition sparked. The jet engine kicked in, turbines roaring as the truck leveled out and zoomed toward Dragon Temple.

Yamcha was certain, if he couldn't get them there on time, no one could...

On the observation deck of the airship, Mai handed Lord Piccolo a Dragon Ball from Goku's pouch.

Piccolo examined it carefully before he placed it on the Dragon Ball altar. The stars within the ball blazed.

"Imagine," Lord Piccolo said, watching the Dragon Balls come to life. "Imagine being shackled so tightly that every atom in your body stood compacted. Still. Even a thought, itself so infinitely small, took a week to wind its way through the labyrinth of a stagnant mind. That was my hell for two thousand years."

Mai handed him another Dragon Ball.

"I survived on a single idea. I fed on it. I will use their own creation to grant me the power to rule their world." He placed another ball on the altar.

Piccolo held the last Dragon Ball tightly in his fist. He turned to Mai, his expression vengeful. "With this Dragon Ball, I reclaim two thousand years and take my vengeance upon the earth!"

Lord Piccolo dropped the last Dragon Ball into place.

The stars within the seven balls aligned.

Slowly, a light began to shine forth, building in intensity until the entire room was imbued with a heavenly glow.

A low rumble was felt from outside the airship. The rumble grew into an explosion. In the plains below the airship, craggy spires made of rock erupted from the ground. A central spire shot up, like a stalk on a giant plant, followed by twisted arches and raised plateaus.

The power of the seven Dragon Balls created the Dragon Temple out of nothing.

Yamcha's utility truck, flying over the once flat

plain, now had to swerve and dip to dodge the shifting earth, the temple springing up all around. Trying his best to avoid the rocks being thrown up into the air, Yamcha held the truck steady as possible. Which wasn't very steady at all.

Bulma was thrown into the passenger door while Goku struggled to keep himself from crushing Roshi.

In the chaos, the containment pot was jostled from Roshi's hands and flew into the back of the truck. The old man dove after it.

Goku focused on the scene ahead, unable to believe his eyes. A Dragon Temple, newly formed out of dirt and rock, stood in glory before him.

The reality of what he was about to face settled heavily in Goku's soul. He reached into the backpack he'd been carrying since the day Lord Piccolo destroyed his home and took his grandpa from him.

Goku pulled out Gohan's orange gi and slipped it on. Next he strapped on Bulma's elbow pads and Yamcha's weapon belt.

Goku was gearing up for the battle of his life. Of all their lives.

On the airship, the blazing light from the Dragon Balls was almost too painful to look at. Lord Piccolo forced his eyes upon the balls as he prepared to recite the prayer of the Dragon Balls.

"The test of seven has been fulfilled," Lord Piccolo began.

In the truck, Roshi, still struggling to regain a hold on the containment pot, looked up the second the dust had finally cleared. He could see Lord Piccolo on the observation deck of the airship beginning the prayer.

Roshi pointed at the airship yelling, "We must stop him before he finishes the prayer."

Yamcha didn't need to know exactly what would happen if they failed. Yamcha cranked the wheel, directing the flying truck right at the ship.

Mai saw it coming and dove for cover as the truck screamed toward the observation deck. Lord Piccolo paused in the middle of the prayer, looking up. Pulling from his own Ki, he shoved a ball of energy at the oncoming truck, effectively knocking it back. The truck twisted, spiraling out of control.

Yamcha wasn't about to give up. With a last-ditch effort, he tugged on a handle, then squeezed a trigger. In the truck bed, a mechanical harpoon-like gun fired.

The metal harpoon struck its target and slammed into the Dragon Ball altar. The collision shook the airship and knocked over the altar, sending Dragon Balls scattering across the floor of the observation deck.

One Dragon Ball fell from the airship and disappeared into the cloud of dust surrounding the Dragon Temple.

Yamcha's truck was finally out of tricks. She was tumbling away from the airship at a pretty good clip. Yamcha tried everything he could think of to stop their fall.

"She's dead," he reported with a sigh.

The indicator needles had all dropped to zero. The power to the jet boosters had failed. He couldn't even restart the engine.

They were feet from the ground and falling fast.

"Bail!" Yamcha shouted. "We have to bail!"

The truck doors flew open as Goku, Yamcha, and Bulma leapt out toward the craggy surfaces below.

Goku crashed down first. Landing on an outcropping above the central spire of Dragon Temple, he rolled, barely stopping himself from going over the edge.

Yamcha and Bulma missed the central spire. Instead, they smashed into a lower terrace of the same building.

Yamcha dove to grab Bulma before she careened off the side and fell to the ground far below.

Only Roshi remained in the truck. Unwilling to leave the carefully crafted containment pot, he had finally reached it in the last few moments before the truck smashed to the ground. Cradling it for safety, Roshi held on tight as Yamcha's truck crashed in a ball of dust and metal.

The remaining Dragon Balls scattered throughout the airship. Lord Piccolo tried to find them, but the chaos of the airship's crash was making that task nearly impossible.

Lord Piccolo knew he'd find the Dragon Balls soon enough. First, there was Goku to reckon with.

"I am glad to have you join me, Kakarrot." Lord Piccolo addressed Goku, who was clinging to the central spire of the Dragon Temple. The Namek's eyes brightened as if he were seeing an old friend. "You will bear witness to my glory when I compel Shen Long to grant me the power to rule this diseased rock you call Earth."

Goku stood. He faced Piccolo. "My name is Goku, and I'm here to destroy you."

Piccolo waved off Goku's decree as if the boy were talking nonsense. "You are a Saiyan. Your true name is

Kakarrot." Piccolo stared firmly at the boy, who didn't flinch under the power of his gaze. "You traveled by meteor to hide amongst the vermin until your eighteenth birthday."

With a sweep of his arm, Piccolo pointed to the crater that had been revealed by the formation of the Dragon Temple. "This is where you landed and where you'll be reborn."

"I don't believe you," Goku said.

Piccolo picked up one of the found Dragon Balls. The stars within it glowed with supernatural light. "Maybe you'll believe the Dragon Ball," he suggested.

Goku's eyes were drawn to the Dragon Ball, as they always were. It was now pulsating in Piccolo's hand. The boy couldn't turn away. It was as if his eyes were glued to the ball and the vision contained therein.

A burning asteroid burrows into the earth. Monstrous red eyes open. In the deep grass a baby cries. Gohan bundles the baby. Its red eyes clear at Gohan's touch.

A stabbing pain shot through Goku's skull. The truth of the vision hitting home.

Lord Piccolo watched the boy intently. "When the blood moon eclipses the sun you will become Oozaru the Destroyer."

Goku was forced to relive the visions he'd had previously, each time he had touched a Dragon Ball. They came cascading through him, clearer than ever before.

The razor sharp fangs. The vicious claws. Oozaru killing his friends.

Goku dropped to his knees. His suffering was extreme.

"Goku is a shell," Lord Piccolo informed him. "Kakarrot, this is who you are."

"Noooo!" Goku screamed, as if fighting against it might somehow make the truth go away.

"There is no denial." Piccolo had no sympathy for the boy. Time was short. "The blood moon is eclipsing the sun."

Above them, the moon was slowly swallowing the sun, the warm rays folding and disappearing around the dark obstruction.

Goku doubled over in pain, sweat beads covering his forehead. He felt his muscles spasm, gripping him tightly as if something inside was fighting to get out.

And his eyes.

Goku's eyes turned red as blood.

"Auuughhhh!" The roar of pain rushed forth from his mouth as teeth, already sharp, glistened in the sun's final rays.

Where once he had a human hand, now claws ripped through his fingers, extending outward.

Bulma and Yamcha were there, shocked to witness their friend's sudden and gruesome transformation.

Drawing his eyes away from Goku, Yamcha noticed something in the crevice of a nearby platform of rock.

A Dragon Ball.

Moving quickly, Yamcha snagged the Dragon Ball. He signaled to Bulma, flashing it at her, inconspicuously, so that Lord Piccolo wouldn't see them. She hustled over and the two of them began to make their way out of the temple. They needed to take that Dragon Ball as far away as possible.

"Oozaru," Lord Piccolo called to the demon. "They have a dragon ball!" Lord Piccolo had seen Yamcha and Bulma locate and collect a Dragon Ball. Piccolo needed that ball. All seven balls had to be together for his wish to come true. He pointed at the pair, frantic to escape the temple compound.

Goku's transformation was complete. There was no

longer any separation between Goku and Oozaru. The destroyer was powerful and deadly.

Oozaru looked down at them. His red eyes blazed.

"Goku, no," Bulma shouted at Oozaru, who headed toward her and Yamcha.

"I don't think Goku's there anymore," Yamcha said, grabbing Bulma's hand and pulling her away.

Oozaru leapt down upon them. With a powerful swipe, he ripped a gash into the stone, narrowly missing Bulma and Yamcha.

The chase began in earnest. Bulma and Yamcha ran desperately into the labyrinth of tunnels and arches that formed the Dragon Temple. But Oozaru was right behind them. With a slash of his monstrous claws, he easily broke through the walls, coming nearer and nearer.

Yamcha and Bulma dashed headlong into an opening in the rocky maze. Oozaru intercepted them, blocking their path, forcing them to stop. In a single, powerful swipe, Oozaru smacked Yamcha across the chest, sending him flying against the temple wall. Yamcha crumpled to the floor and the Dragon Ball in his hand flew into the air. Bulma caught it like a well-trained wide receiver.

She then took out her weapon and unloaded

everything she had on Oozaru. Bullets exploded on the destroyer's body and the force knocked him down, temporarily stunning him. But he got right back up again.

Bulma took advantage of the small amount of time that Oozaru was down to sprint out of the maze.

Outside the temple, the wreckage of Yamcha's utility truck rested in an unrecognizable heap of twisted metal. A cracking sound echoed through the valley, as a side window smashed from the inside out. Roshi, battered and bruised, crawled out through the shattered window.

Gathering his strength, Roshi leapt into the air, up toward the airship.

Piccolo was caught unaware. He turned in surprise as Roshi came at him, like a blasting rocket, holding a blue ball of energy.

Piccolo raised his own hands in defense. A powerful red ball of energy immediately formed. He managed to get the first strike, hurling the energy at Roshi, effectively smashing the old man to the ground.

Bulma emerged from the temple just in time to see Piccolo's attack on Roshi. She ran to help the old master, and in that same moment Oozaru appeared from within the rocky maze.

Lord Piccolo called to Oozaru, "Get the Dragon Ball. Kill them all!"

Oozaru leapt down from the arched terrace, landing with a bang near where Bulma was helping Roshi to his feet.

Upon seeing the demon headed toward them, Roshi grabbed Bulma and the two of them hustled toward where the airship hovered, so they were out of Lord Piccolo's sight.

Oozaru was moving fast and Roshi knew the end was near.

Lord Piccolo stood watching the events unfold from the airship observation deck. Mai was there, by his side.

Oozaru was focused on the old man. It seemed that the woman with the Dragon Ball was going to get away. The Namek had to do something. And fast.

"I'll get it myself," Lord Piccolo declared, his frustration mounting. Determined to get back his Dragon Ball, he leapt over the observation deck of the airship, dropping down to the ground below.

Coming face to face with Lord Piccolo was exactly what Roshi had hoped for. In one smooth movement, he slid the containment pot under the path of Piccolo as he fell to the ground. It would take all of his life force to finish the job...

"Ma Fu Ba!!" Master Roshi declared.

Fire from the bowels of the earth shot through the ground and burned all the way to the heavens. Water from deep underground aquifers burst through the soil. The air above swirled into a funnel. All three elements rushed into Roshi, carving a path through his emblazoned body.

Energy exploded from Master Roshi as the Ma Fu Ba was cast. The powerful curse encircled Lord Piccolo, who realized too late that he was trapped. The curse was so powerful storm clouds formed and coiled about the Namekian demon.

The clouds reached out, like hands, twisting and tumbling, dragging the Namek down.

"Ahhhhh!" Lord Piccolo screamed.

That scream was the last sound Lord Piccolo uttered before he was sucked into the containment pot.

# CHAPTER FOURTEEN

When Mai saw the containment pot, the lid tightly sealed, she immediately brought out a long barrel pistol from her waist, took aim and fired. The bullet drilled the containment pot, not shattering it, but causing a crack to form.

The crack spread, forming a spider web of weak spots in the clay. All eyes were glued to the container.

With a shout that could be heard in the four corners of the earth, Lord Piccolo exploded out of his containment.

Roshi had failed. Piccolo was free and the containment pot, so carefully constructed with the prayers of many monks, shattered to a million pieces.

Master Roshi had expended every ounce of life to perform the Ma Fu Ba. His time had come. He lay on the temple ground. His breaths were shallow. Darkness covered his eyes as Roshi's death neared.

Tucked inside a barely audible gasp, he had but one

thing to say to Bulma.

"Run."

Tears flowed from her eyes as Bulma looked to where Roshi's eyes were trained. Oozaru the Destroyer approached. Bulma took the man's advice and ran.

Roshi was going to hold Oozaru back. Protect her until the very end.

When Oozaru was close enough, the old man called out to the demon with the last of his strength.

Oozaru drew near, reaching down toward the old man's neck, ready to crush the life out of him. Even as Roshi battled to retain consciousness, he found it within him to lock eyes with Oozaru.

A tiny spark ignited in Roshi's hand as Roshi reached up and touched the demon.

Oozaru flinched. His blood red eyes began to clear.

"Oozaru can't be beaten with fists," Roshi told the boy within the monster. "Only with faith can you win. Don't let Oozaru destroy the Goku in you."

Goku's eyes cleared fully as Roshi exhaled his last breath.

Oozaru screamed with a sorrow so deep that it could only have come from Goku himself. As if in pain, Oozaru struck the earth, pounding the rocky walls.

Goku was fighting to get out, and with each impact

of fist against rock a little more of him was revealed. Finally, with a last painful slam against the ground, Oozaru became Goku again.

"Impossible!" Lord Piccolo exclaimed, having witnessed Goku's return. "No Saiyan has ever reverted to human form before."

Goku felt stronger than he'd ever felt. "Something I learned from my grandfather: First rule is...there are no rules."

Piccolo angrily lunged at Goku.

"Goku!" Bulma tossed Gohan's bow staff to her friend.

"Thanks," Goku replied as he snatched the pole from the air. He whipped the staff around, ready to take on Lord Piccolo.

While Goku and Piccolo's fight raged, Mai focused on Bulma.

Her alien weapon aimed, Mai fired multiple bursts at Bulma while dodging the returning fire. Bulma, hanging on to the single Dragon Ball for dear life, dashed back into the temple maze. Mai followed.

Lord Piccolo blocked each of Goku's attacks strike for strike. Goku was wielding the bow staff with amazing speed, the power pole blazing. The staff struck at Piccolo high and low, but the alien countered each blow easily, treating the staff like a minor annoyance.

"Nyoibo extend!" Goku thrust the bow staff forward, its full length shooting out.

Avoiding the onslaught, Piccolo merely arched back, wrapping his left arm around the pole. With his right hand, Piccolo chopped through the power pole as if it were a toothpick. Gohan's bow staff was broken in two.

Piccolo was now on the offensive. His punches cracked like thunder. Goku was kicked into the air then kicked again into a temple pillar. Goku slid down the rocky rubble in a daze.

Bulma wasn't doing much better in the temple maze. She opened fire on Mai. But Mai was fast and rolled out of the way, coming back at Bulma with a wicked spray of bullets.

A portion of the half-wall Bulma was hiding behind was blown to bits. Bulma got up, determination in her eyes, and began to run down the rocky tunnel, firing as she moved, but missing her target every time.

Goku launched himself at Piccolo, moving so fast that

he appeared to be in four places at once. It still wasn't enough.

Every punch that Goku threw, Lord Piccolo matched. Piccolo hit Goku with a slash and an elbow that snapped Goku's head back. A twisting sweep kick crushed Goku's ribs. And in a final blow, Goku was kicked so hard that he was burrowed into the ground, battered and weary.

Bulma hit the dirt face first when the wall behind her exploded. She opened fire, coming round a corner, fully expecting to find Mai in the tunnel. But the tunnel was empty.

Confused, Bulma looked around the darkened space. A sound. A clink and a roll. Then a low hiss.

Bulma saw the high-tech grenade tumbling toward her in the tunnel. She had no time to think. She got up and ran toward an opening behind her. The grenade exploded. Flames bloomed like a red flower as the concussion rippled the air.

Bulma dove out of a tunnel opening and crashed to the ground onto another level of the temple as the explosion ricocheted behind her. On impact the Dragon Ball that she'd been so carefully protecting was knocked from her hand.

The Dragon Ball rolled down the temple terraces,

bouncing over cracks and rocks until finally coming to rest in a tiny crater halfway between Piccolo and Goku.

Lord Piccolo dove for it first. Goku was behind him, and in a masterful martial arts move, delivered the Shadow Crane Strike, knocking the Dragon Ball away from Piccolo's reach.

Furious, Piccolo went for it again, and this time, Goku shoved the Dragon Ball away with his Ki.

It was Goku's turn to go for it. He was inches from the Dragon Ball when Lord Piccolo played the same game. He sent his Ki cascading, blowing Goku twenty feet away and leaving a crater where Goku had just been.

"Humans can never hope to defeat me," Lord Piccolo declared, his voice echoing through the rocky landscape of the Dragon Temple.

Goku pulled himself up on his hands and knees. "I am …Goku … I am… Oozaru." He stood fully upright. "To be at one with myself, I must be two."

Goku closed his eyes, concentrating. Suddenly, he screamed. His mouth opened to reveal fangs. His body filled with power. His muscles bulked up.

Goku then opened his eyes. They burned red with fire. The transformation wasn't entirely complete however. Goku wasn't Oozaru, but he was more than Goku alone. He took the Shadow Crane Form.

"I must…have faith in who I am." Goku sent out his Ki from his hand. The powerful force traveled through the air, sucking the energy from the elements. It struck Piccolo, smashing him into the central spire of Dragon Temple.

The demon angrily pulled himself out of the rubble. He sent a tsunami wave of energy back at Goku, while advancing on him at the same time.

Goku dodged and rolled past the explosions. The air around him filled with dust and debris. Red eyes blazing, Goku lashed out at Piccolo.

The enemies collided.

Bulma had been battered by the explosion and Mai knew it. She stood over Bulma, her weapon ready. One squeeze of the trigger, and Bulma would be finished.

Suddenly, Mai dropped to the ground. It wasn't Bulma who was done, it was Mai. Yamcha had taken her down with a shuriken throwing knife.

"Nice throw," Bulma told Yamcha, who had just saved her life.

"Thanks," Yamcha said, just before he collapsed in the sand, completely exhausted.

It was time for Goku to end his battle with Lord Piccolo.

"Ma Fu Ba!" Goku pulled his hands back to his waist, summoning all the energy from his surroundings. Fire erupted from the ground. Water burst from the aquifer. The air twisted and turned. All three elements funneled into Goku.

The boy screamed as the force of the elements tore through him.

Piccolo sneered at Goku's feeble attempt to channel his Ki. In his hand, an orb of red energy formed. "Human power has failed before as it will again." Using all his forces, Piccolo shot his blazing ball of energy at Goku.

"Kame-hame-ha!" Goku shouted just as the moon eclipsed the sun.

A green flash rippled out from the eclipsed sun. Its energy joined the three elements from the earth. Alien and earthly powers funneled through Goku into his hands. A bolt of light formed which Goku sent hurling toward Piccolo.

The Namekian Lord recoiled in surprise and fear as his life forces were extinguished by the sum of the alien and the human: Goku and Oozaru.

As Piccolo fell, the Dragon Ball slipped from his grasp.

# CHAPTER FIFTEEN

The sun escaped the blood moon. The eclipse was over.

Goku and Bulma joined Yamcha near Roshi's inert body. As sunlight spread over the Dragon Temple, the three stood over Master Roshi. The sun would not change his death.

"I wish it didn't have to end this way," Bulma said, eyes full of tears. The Dragon Ball from Lord Piccolo's hand rolled to Goku's feet. Goku looked at it and picked it up. "Shen Long," he said softly. "One wish will be granted."

In the Dragon Temple, Yamcha, Bulma, and Goku brought together six Dragon Balls. Goku slowly and ceremoniously approached with the seventh. It was the four-star ball his grandfather had given him for his eighteenth birthday.

Goku set Sushinchu in its proper place.

The stars within the balls aligned. Brilliantly they glowed, building in intensity until the entire room was imbued with a heavenly light.

Goku recited the prayer. "Dragon, the test of seven has been fulfilled. I compel you to come forth and grant my wish."

The Dragon Balls flew high into the air, spinning rapidly, shooting rays of light out into the heavens until all seven merged and became one light.

Shen Long, the Dragon, appeared in the sky, his light so intense Bulma and Yamcha had to shield their eyes. Goku, however, was entranced and able to look up to the Dragon.

"Give life to Muten-Roshi," Goku requested.

Shen Long roared and from the dragon's mouth, a light spiraled down into Roshi. His lifeless body filled with energy. Color returned to his skin. And Roshi gasped a new breath. Life was restored.

The light faded. Shen Long returned to his place in the sky. The seven spinning Dragon Balls suddenly repelled one another and in a blink they flew away, disappearing to the four corners of the earth.

"I had the strangest dream," Master Roshi said as Goku and Bulma helped him sit up. "I was in a place I can't describe, but I felt content. Like I belonged. I was happy." He turned to Goku. "Then your grandfather Gohan came up to me and kicked me out. Said there was a lot you still needed to learn."

Goku laughed. "Grandpa was right. I'm sorry Master Roshi, we weren't ready to have you leave us."

Roshi smiled. "I know he's right. I wasn't ready to go."

Yamcha was overcome by the emotion between Roshi and Goku. Not. "That's sweet, ladies," he teased them. "But did you notice we're missing something?"

Goku looked around at his friend and shrugged. He felt complete.

Bulma explained. "The Dragon Balls are gone. We have to find them again. You ready?"

Goku would follow his friends to the ends of the earth to find and gather the Dragon Balls, but he wasn't quite ready to begin the quest just yet.

"I have to do one thing," he told them. "One important thing."

# EPILOGUE

Chi Chi was in the Toi San Temple practicing her form. Her movements were graceful and fluid. Suddenly, she stopped, mid-move, as if sensing something.

Chi Chi turned, and her face lit up to find Goku standing nearby. She ran to him and wrapped her arms around him, hugging him as if she'd never let him go.

"I didn't know if I would see you again," she said when at last she pulled back, taking a good long look at him.

"I'm sorry. I'm so sorry I hurt you," Goku told her, heart full of emotion. "I would never do it on purpose. It was in the heat of battle and...I thought you were someone else."

"It's all right," Chi Chi said with a smile. "I let you hit me."

"I was just too fast," Goku retorted.

"You're fast," she countered, "but I let you hit me."

"It was dark and confusing and..."

"Whoa." She put up a hand to stop him. "If our relationship is going anywhere we're going to have to settle this."

The twosome met on the battle stage; Chi Chi in one corner, Goku in the other. They bowed politely to each other, then assumed their poses. Smiles turned up the corners of their mouths. Leaping into the air, each was ready to strike...